Eliza Orne White

A Browning Courtship and other Stories

Eliza Orne White

A Browning Courtship and other Stories

ISBN/EAN: 9783743322196

Manufactured in Europe, USA, Canada, Australia, Japa

Cover: Foto ©ninafisch / pixelio.de

Manufactured and distributed by brebook publishing software (www.brebook.com)

Eliza Orne White

A Browning Courtship and other Stories

Books by Eliza Orne White.

WINTERBOROUGH. A Novel. 16mo, $1.25; paper, 50 cents.

THE COMING OF THEODORA. A Novel. 16mo, $1.25.

WHEN MOLLY WAS SIX. A Book for Children. With Colored Cover Design and other Illustrations. Square 12mo, $1.00.

A LITTLE GIRL OF LONG AGO. A Book for Children. With Colored Cover Design and other Illustrations. Square 12mo, $1.00.

A BROWNING COURTSHIP AND OTHER STORIES. 16mo, $1.25.

HOUGHTON, MIFFLIN & CO.
BOSTON AND NEW YORK.

A BROWNING COURTSHIP

And Other Stories

BY

ELIZA ORNE WHITE

BOSTON AND NEW YORK
HOUGHTON, MIFFLIN AND COMPANY
The Riverside Press, Cambridge
1897

CONTENTS

	PAGE
A Browning Courtship	1
Commonplace Carrie	51
A Bismarck Dinner	102
A Hamerton Type-Writer	119
A Faithful Failure	142
The Queen of Clubs	190
The Fatted Calf	217
Two Authors	248

"Commonplace Carrie" and "A Hamerton Type-Writer" are reprinted from *The New England Magazine*, and "The Fatted Calf" from *Harper's Bazar*, by permission of the publishers.

A BROWNING COURTSHIP

MAY 25. I am twenty years old to-day! I used to think that the first fresh bloom of one's youth was over at twenty; but I have reached that advanced **period** without even beginning to have any **fun**. I don't see what use there is in my being young and pretty, when there is nobody any more exciting than Miss Niles to tell me that **I am so**. I wish I knew some young men! **I am** fully aware how heterodox this sentiment is considered, but I repeat it boldly, and even underline it, — *I should like to know some interesting men!*

Just at this point mamma called to me from below, "May, dear, don't you want to cut the asparagus for me?" In order to live up to the standard of truth that my mother advocates, I should have replied promptly, "No, dear, I don't;" but I have all my life disguised my real sentiments beneath a veil of apparent cheerfulness and amiability; so I took the basket and knife, and descended to the garden. Mamma little knows how rebellious I am at heart, and how I hate this dull, quiet life. I should like to know whether the society in all small New England towns consists chiefly of maiden ladies, of all varieties and ages. The Northbridge maiden ladies are very nice, but they all have a more or less resigned expression. I wonder at what period they definitely gave up the hope of knowing any interesting men.

Miss Niles was in her garden cutting asparagus, too. She bobbed her long pale face forward, so that she could see me through the hole in the hedge. She looks queerer than ever since she has taken to wearing that green sun-bonnet; but she is so good that I ought not to make fun of her.

"Good-morning, May," she said in her slow, sentimental way. "How fresh and beautiful you look, and like the sweet month for which you are named! Do you remember those lines of Browning?" and she began a quotation, brandishing the asparagus knife in the air.

I never remember any poetry, and Browning is my especial aversion, but I smiled and said, "How lovely!" in the proper places.

"I am glad you care so intensely for Browning, dearest May," Miss Niles said; "you are a great satisfaction to my soul. You too feel the charm and depth of meaning in his lightest words. I recollect how deeply you enjoyed 'Childe Roland' and 'Paracelsus,' and I am going to read you 'The Red Cotton Night-Cap Country.'"

I contrived to hide the feelings caused by this announcement, and said politely, "You are very kind, and I shall be glad to hear anything that you choose to read, only — I don't think I wholly understand Browning yet."

"No one comprehends him at first, dear; the knowledge comes later, after much hard work and perseverance, like — like — the love of olives."

Miss Niles never knows how she is

going to end a sentence when she begins it, and the result is sometimes startling.

There was a pause, during which we both cut asparagus assiduously, and then she began again:—

"You have such a true appreciation of the spirit of Browning's poetry that we have voted you into our club, although you are so much younger than the other members. Think what an honor!"

Just then I could not but admit that there was something to be said on the side of those persons who advocate perfect truth in all the relations of life, but it was too late to retreat. Had n't I sat for the whole of a long spring afternoon, in apparent rapt contemplation, as she read me page after page, each more incomprehensible than the last; while my thoughts refused to conform to any effort of my will, but flew vaguely from one inappropriate theme to another? And all because I could not bear to hurt her feelings!

"I suppose you have heard of our wonderful good fortune," said Miss Niles, leaning forward, and once more peeping at me through the hedge. "Paul Brown, the distinguished P. K. Brown, who is such a great Browning scholar, is coming to spend the summer here, and we hope to persuade him to conduct our study class."

"Indeed!" I exclaimed. "How delightful!" and my unworthy mind immediately busied itself in conjectures as to the age of Mr. P. K. Brown.

"He is a young man of great talent," Miss Niles continued. "They say the amount of knowledge that he has on the subject is really wonderful, considering that he is n't more than four or five and twenty. There comes the butter-man; how provoking! But we will talk this matter over another time."

Miss Niles kissed her hand to me and departed, trailing her black wrapper along the gravel path, and making the transition from Browning to butter with preternatural dignity.

I was left to my own reflections, which were of a mixed nature.

When the gods grant the requests of mortals, do they always hamper the fulfillment with some condition that sends leanness into their souls? I asked myself. Only ten minutes before I had been wishing that I knew some young men, and now this P. K. Brown, of four or five and twenty, was about to descend among us, but, as if by the irony of fate, devoted to his odious Browning, and consequently talking and thinking in a jargon with which I have not the smallest sympathy.

May 30. I have seen him go by the house, and he has one of the most charming faces imaginable: not handsome, precisely, but intellectual, with dark eyes full of expression, and an adorable brown mustache. I have decided to join the Browning Class.

June 3. Heaven forgive me for my sins! I have told Mr. P. K. Brown that I am an enthusiast over Browning! It would be possible to extenuate my conduct by saying that I was driven into it, but I scorn to take refuge in such a subterfuge. I will at least be wholly sincere with myself. This is how it happened:—

Miss Niles had an evening reception for Piquet (I can't resist calling him so, and making one word of it), and all the aristocracy of Northbridge was present, numbering fifty ladies and six gentlemen. Miss Niles was so busy that she forgot to introduce Mr. Brown to me, and he was immediately seized upon by Mrs. Jansen. I could catch a glimpse of his poetical face over her broad shoulders, and I wondered whether she would keep him to herself all the evening.

I don't like receptions. The wrong people always stick to you like burrs, and the right ones have only time to say a word in passing. For instance, I really love Annie Fairchild, but she would hardly speak to me, for she was bent upon a missionary tour, as usual, and so departed to make herself agreeable to some forlorn person. By the way, why is n't it just as untruthful to pretend to enjoy stupid people as it is to appear to care for poetry that you dislike? I told Annie that I thought her very insincere, but she only laughed and went her mistaken way, not minding in the least that she left me to the tender mercies of Colonel Parminter, who is without exception the greatest bore I know. There is a limit to endurance, and this limit was reached when the colonel began to tell me for the fiftieth time his tale about the narrow escape he had at the battle of Bull Run.

"I am afraid I have perhaps told you this story before, my dear young friend," he observed, "but you are so sympathetic."

"A good story is always worth hearing a second time," I said, blandly; "but if you will pardon me, I suppose I ought to go and help Miss Niles pass the cake and lemonade."

"Certainly, certainly, my dear young friend," said the colonel, nodding his silvery head with antiquated courtesy.

I went the rounds of the room. Most of the people selected their cake with as much deliberation as if it were a solemn duty. Annie took some caraway-seed cookies, for fear there would not be enough cake to go around. Colonel Parminter, on the contrary, picked out some cocoanut cakes and macaroons, with consequential gravity. I prefer his plan to

Annie's, for I do not believe that you will benefit the world any more than yourself by being self-sacrificing. For it is quite probable that, after fasting virtuously on caraway-seed cookies, you will discover that your neighbor has been secretly longing to feast on them, whereas, owing to your unnecessary self-immolation, there are none left. As with caraway-seed cookies, so with life.

Annie might avoid Mr. P. K. Brown as much as she liked, but I was not made in that mould. I proceeded to pass him the cake. He was very animated, and apparently much interested in talking with Miss Anderson. He put out his hand to make some explanatory motion, and hit the cake-basket, sending three cookies flying in different directions. Then he looked up. Our eyes met. I shall never forget how his face changed when he saw me. He glanced at me first with glad surprise, probably because I was the youngest person in the room; but afterwards he gave me a curious, satisfied look, as if he had been expecting me always, and found me at last. I flushed under his keen scrutiny. The mutual embarrassment lasted only a moment, for he almost instantly stooped to pick up the cookies.

"What shall I do with them?" he asked helplessly.

"We will eat them," I replied audaciously. "Miss Niles's floor is always as clean as a plate. Won't you have one, Miss Anderson?" I added wickedly.

"No, thank you," she said, seeming greatly shocked. "To return to the Old Pictures in Florence, Mr. Brown. I shall be pleased to have you come and inspect my collection, and select those that are necessary for the illustration and elucidation of our first study lesson."

Miss Anderson always talks like a dictionary. I really cannot do her justice.

She surveyed me critically. I was sure she noticed that my bang did not curl as well as usual, and that my pink cashmere gown was my old white one dyed. I smiled back at her in my sweetest manner, yet in my heart I thought how gladly she would give her maroon satin in exchange for my dyed cashmere, if only she could throw her extra fifteen years in to balance the account. I don't like Harriet Anderson. Just then Miss Niles came up. "Talking about the Florentine pictures? How delightful!" she said. "Mr. Brown, have you been presented to my dear young friend, Miss Cheney? She is one of the most hopeful and promising of our Browning enthusiasts." At this point Miss Anderson raised her eyebrows. She looked at me coldly and most disagreeably. Her glance decided me.

"Yes," I said, "I am very fond of Browning's poetry, only I do not pretend to know much about him."

"No?" said Miss Anderson. "I am glad you make no pretenses."

This insulting speech roused me to fresh untruths. "I know very little about him," I reiterated, "but I care so much for some of his things that I am anxious to read as much of him as possible."

I felt so virtuous while I was saying this, so truthful and innocent, and as if I really were the appreciative young person that I knew Mr. Brown thought me, my words were so modest and my tones so truly convincing, that even Miss Anderson looked baffled.

"Do you belong to the Browning Class, Miss Cheney?" asked the hero.

What a pleasant voice he has! I thought. He will be sure to read well. Perhaps I shall really get to like Browning.

"Yes," I replied with enthusiasm, for Miss Anderson's eye was still upon me, "I am happy to say that I have just had the good fortune to be chosen a member."

Now I have told the whole disgraceful truth, and I have no doubt that Mr. Brown will begin the study lessons cheered by the thought that there is one congenial spirit in the class, who is as wildly devoted to Browning as he is himself. Well, it's too late for regrets. I am in for it now.

June 7. The Browning Club met for the first time last night. The subject was Old Pictures in Florence, but we only got through the first verse.

Mr. Brown began: —

A BROWNING COURTSHIP

"'The morn when first it thunders in March,
The eel in the pond gives a leap, they say'"—
but at this point he was interrupted by Colonel Parminter, who wanted to know the reason why. He was very serious about it, and to look at him you would have said that the fate of nations depended upon the correct solution of the problem.

"That is n't what I call poetry," said little Miss Perkins in her high-pitched voice. "The lines are very unmusical, and then who cares to know whether the eel leaps in the pond or not?" But she was instantly frowned down.

"My dear madam, it is a matter of the utmost importance that we understand each line perfectly before we proceed to the next," observed the colonel.

"Yes," assented Miss Niles. "Do you consider that passage allegorical, Mr. Brown? Does the leaping of the eel in the pond symbolize the struggles of Italy for liberty?"

"I will get the encyclopædia and look up eels," said Mrs. Ellis. "I should like to know whether all eels leap in all ponds when it first thunders, or whether this habit is peculiar to Italy."

"Don't you think it is just a local superstition," suggested Annie mildly, "and had n't we better go on to the more important part of the poem?"

"It is all equally important," said Colonel Parminter gravely. "Each word that Browning ever wrote is of equal importance with every other word."

Just then Mrs. Ellis came back with the encyclopædia, opened at Ichthyology.

"My dear friends," she exclaimed enthusiastically, "I had no idea that fishes were so interesting! Come and look at this picture of a trigger fish, and at this queer creature with a fluted collar. See, Grace, its eyes are stilted out from its head on a cartilaginous stem! How convenient it would be to have that arrangement of eyes when we are driving with your father, and he wants us to look at all the things that are just behind us!" and Mrs. Ellis laughed gayly.

We all joined in; it was a relief to find something that we were expected to laugh at.

A BROWNING COURTSHIP

Then Grace asked, "Hadn't you better skip the cuttle fishes and their relations, mother, and proceed to eels? It is very interesting, but we didn't form the class to study fishes."

Mrs. Ellis followed her suggestion obediently.

"See here, girls," she said, looking abstractedly at Colonel Parminter; "the town of Ely, in England, is said to be so named from the rents having been formerly paid in eels, and Elmore"—

"Does it say anything about the eel leaping in the pond, Mrs. Ellis?" asked the colonel. He spoke with that severe air of superiority which even the least wise of the opposite sex feels it incumbent upon him to assume over ours, if we chance to wander from the subject when he would like the floor himself.

"Electrical eels!" continued Mrs. Ellis. "*They* are so interesting. Listen to this: 'These eels are captured by driving horses and mules into the water, the electric powers of the fish being first exhausted and'"—

"I have it!" cried Miss Niles sud-

A BROWNING COURTSHIP

denly. "The explanation of the eel leaping in the thunder-storm has come to me in an electric flash. They are *electric* eels, and so when there is electricity in the air they rise to meet it, as the magnet seek the iron. Isn't this conformable with the laws of electricity, Mr. Brown?"

Piquet kept a straight face. "It is a very ingenious explanation," he said politely, "but, unfortunately, I believe the electric eels are found only in South America."

"Supposing we proceed to the next line," suggested Colonel Parminter (even his patience was giving way, it seemed), "and appoint a committee to look up the subject of eels for our next meeting."

His motion was cheerfully carried, and Mr. Brown began again:—

"'The morn when first it thunders in March,
The eel in the pond gives a leap, they say.
As I leaned and looked over the aloed arch
Of the villa gate this warm March day,
No flash snapt, no dum thunder rolled'"—

"What on earth is dumb thunder?" broke in Miss Perkins, who had n't seen the spelling of the word. "Of all out-

A BROWNING COURTSHIP

landish expressions, that is the queerest. I should think even Browning would have more sense than that. Dumb thunder! Dumb lightning might be allowed, although peculiar; but dumb thunder!"

Mrs. Ellis flew to the dictionary, only to find that "d-u-m" was not in it, and Colonel Parminter began a vivid description of a battle, telling us how the roar of the artillery sounded like a severe thunder-storm. This reminded Miss Niles of a time in her youth when the house next to her own was struck by lightning. At this point Mrs. Jansen pounded on the table to call us to order, as Mr. Brown was too polite to interfere with us.

The last line of the first verse of our choice poem is: —

"Florence lay out on the mountain side;"

and so we were put through a series of tedious photographs, and made familiar with the map of Florence. I begin to wish that I had *not* joined the Browning Class.

June 15. Last night the club met again. After the lesson was over, Mr.

A BROWNING COURTSHIP

Brown came up to me, while I was putting on my things, and asked if he might have the pleasure of walking home with me.

"You may," I replied, smiling. "It is the one object of my life to give pleasure."

"Then you certainly attain your ideal, which is more than most of us can say."

As he spoke he gave me a grave, flattering glance of approval.

The moon was shining brightly, and the scent of roses was in the air as we passed through Mrs. Jansen's porch. We could hear the sound of loud voices and laughter from the house behind us, where the club were putting on their wraps and overshoes; but in front of us was quite a different world, silver, and mysterious in its perfumed beauty. Even I was impressed by it.

"What a night!" exclaimed Mr. Brown, as if sure of my sympathy.

We had barely reached the gate when we heard voices behind us, and presently Miss Niles's slow soprano. "Where is May Chency?" she inquired. "I promised I would see her home, and I can't find her, and I am afraid to go alone."

"I had forgotten all about Miss Niles," I said, pausing, conscience-stricken. "I must go back for her."

I was full of apologies, and Mr. Brown offered his arm to her with the same quiet charm of manner that he had shown me.

"Exquisite moon!" exclaimed Miss Niles. "I am glad the rain is over. A truly poetic moon, is it not, Mr. Brown? I shouldn't have been so long, only I couldn't find one of my rubbers."

Poor Miss Niles! In spite of my long acquaintance with her, I never cease to be surprised by her abrupt changes of subject.

July 5. We have Browning two evenings a week now. The more frivolous members of the club have begged for some of the lighter selections; so there is the study class, which is still upon Old Pictures, every Tuesday night, and on Thursday evening Piquet gives us what he chooses. Annie enjoys everything he reads, intensely, and does not show it; and I don't enjoy everything, and don't show it. *Voilà* the difference. We are each deceitful after our own fashion. If Mr. Brown knew what was good for him, he would fall in love with her, even although she is twenty-seven and he only twenty-four; but he has been indiscreet enough to — I am not sure of it, so I won't write it down, but it is pleasant. Not that I especially care about him, for he is too serious and conscientious to suit my taste, and then Browning will always be his absorbing passion.

July 25. Miss Niles is indefatigable. She proposes that we shall act "Colombe's Birthday," I to be Colombe. I should die of it, there is so much to learn; and I never could commit poetry, even when at school. Besides, there are seven men in the play, and we can muster only Mr. Brown, Colonel Parminter, and Mr. Seabury.

August 5. The hot wave has mercifully come, and we are all too limp to think of acting, but are to read "Colombe's Birthday" instead.

September 1. It is very provoking. I am never at home when Mr. Brown calls; this is the third time I have missed him. On the contrary, I am invariably in when Miss Niles or the colonel appears. Such is the contrariness of **fate**!

To-night, after the class, Piquet complained that he never sees me now.

"You have that pleasure every Tuesday and Thursday evening. I should think that was enough for any reasonable being," I observed.

"Perhaps I am not a reasonable being," he said in a low tone.

"Well, I am," I returned lightly.

"Then, what satisfaction is there in seeing you among a crowd of people?" he asked.

But, as might have been expected, just then two of the crowd interrupted us. They were full of "Sordello," which Miss Anderson is determined we shall study next.

October 1. Mr. P. K. Brown is going into uncle John's office, so he will stay here indefinitely; certainly all winter, and longer if they like each other.

October 5. I have begun to make a Browning Calendar for a Christmas pre-

A BROWNING COURTSHIP

sent for Mr. Brown. I think there could not be a greater proof of friendly regard than that, and he seems to want proofs. Of course I like him! If I did n't, would I write out three hundred and sixty-five deep quotations, each more stupid than the last? I wish he did not like Browning so well; but he shall have a portion of him for every day in the year.

December 25. Paul Kent Brown has given me a whole set of Browning bound in white vellum! What reckless extravagance! And for the same amount of money he might have given me a gold bangle and a silver-headed umbrella, and ever so many other things I want!

January 8. It has come at last. I do not understand why men are such fools! Why could not Paul Brown have gone on quietly with our pleasant, peaceful friendship? For it was pleasant, a very, very pleasant — flirtation? Well, malevolent beings like Miss Anderson may say that I flirted, if they choose. I wonder just what a flirtation is. I should like to fly to Mrs. Ellis's encyclopædia and look it up. I do not see why they

A BROWNING COURTSHIP

never put interesting articles in the encyclopædia. The dictionary says, "Playing at courtship," and I certainly never did " play at courtship,"— never, never! I defy Miss Anderson, and Mrs. Jansen, and all the rest of them, to say that I did. If I made Paul Brown think I liked him better than I really did, as he says, why, one never expects to be taken so seriously. Of course I like him, and do now, in spite of his having been such an idiot, only — But I will write out the whole scene, that I may see clearly how I have not been in the least to blame. If Miss Anderson had not told him that I was a flirt, it would not have happened; and her accusation was absurd, as I have never had any one to flirt with.

I was skating with Annie, and we were trying to teach Miss Niles, who used to skate a little when she was a girl, which was so long ago that she has forgotten how. Miss Niles looks more gaunt and grim on the ice than anywhere else, poor dear. Paul Brown soon joined us, and asked us if we did not want to go up the river a mile or two, and see the huge fire that the boys had made on the ice. Miss Niles couldn't, and Annie, with her mistaken idea of self-sacrifice, stayed with her, although I was dying to have her come with me, and cast beseeching glances at her.

Paul and I skated on for some moments in silence. Paul skates delightfully, and his fine figure shows off to especial advantage on the ice. At last he said abruptly, "I cannot stand this sort of thing any longer."

"Can't you?" I asked, instantly turning and facing the other way. "Then we will go back to Miss Niles."

"May," he said, in a certain masculine fashion of his own that is not to be withstood, "I won't be played with any longer. You must know that I, at least, am in earnest."

My heart beat very fast, and I did not reply at first. Then I answered, "I don't know what more you want. I'm sure I like you very much, almost as well as I like Annie Fairchild; and I, at least, am in earnest," I added, imitating his tones and skating rapidly on.

He caught up with me in a moment. I should think he might have taken these hints, and been satisfied to let the matter pass off lightly; but he was n't, and there was not the slightest use in trying to stop him.

"I wish you would skate on as fast as you can," I said, "for I want to get to the fire. I am cold."

"You never spoke a truer word," he rejoined; "you *are* cold," and then he began to quote Browning.

I have verified the quotation in my white-vellumed edition, and, although it is not especially flattering, I will put it in : —

"'But for loving, why you would not, sweet,
  Though we prayed you,
  Paid you, brayed you in a mortar,
  For you could not, sweet.'"

He said this verse between his teeth, in rather a savage fashion; and then — oh, dear! I can't remember all that happened, and if I could I would not write it down; only he was not satisfied, even after I had turned serious and talked sensibly.

I don't see why men want to have things so definite! It is one thing to have a man nice to you, and quite another thing to promise to marry him. Why, I don't want to be married for ten years, at least. I don't know that I ever want to be married. I merely wished to know some interesting men, and now — now — Of course we shall be just as good friends as ever.

January 15. Paul Brown never seems to see me at the Browning Class. When he reads, he looks over in the corner where Annie Fairchild and Grace Ellis are sitting, and when I bow to him and try to say something pleasant, he merely nods coldly. I don't see why a man need be rude to a girl, just because she does not want to be engaged to him! There are plenty of men in the world a great deal nicer than Mr. Paul Kent Brown, and some day I shall know them.

January 28. I do not pretend to understand men. I am sure, if I had been as foolishly in love as Paul Brown gave me to understand that he was, I should n't get all over it in three weeks, and be so uncivil that everybody notices it. Not that he does anything; he just does n't do anything. Only he used to look at me as *if* — and now he looks at me as IF — that's all; but there is sometimes a vast difference in an "if." Well, I'm glad I don't care about him.

February 1. Paul Brown is just as nice to Annie as he can be, and lovely to Grace, perfectly devoted to her. To be sure, she is thirty-three, but one sometimes hears of such marriages. Oh, dear! not that I care; only I wish there were somebody that I could be devoted to, — I should like to see how he would enjoy that; but there is nobody except Colonel Parminter, and as he is sixty years old he does n't count.

March 1. I wish Miss Anderson would not say such hateful things. She was talking to Mr. Brown at the post-office, the other day, when I went to get my mail, and as I passed she stopped me.

"Good morning, May," she said. "How are you? I was sorry that you were unable to attend the Browning Class the other night. You are looking wretchedly; you've lost all your roses."

This speech was meant for Paul Brown's ears, and he showed such interest that it brought all my roses back. It vexes me that I have not got over my school-girl trick of blushing.

I turned and faced the two. "I am very well, thank you. I stayed away entirely out of consideration for the class, and not on my own account, for I had such a troublesome cough that I knew it would annoy you all."

Miss Anderson looked at me as if she believed that my cough was a fiction, but it was n't. I don't see why she is always suspecting me of being untruthful. I should think Paul Brown might have walked home with me, but he did n't. I do not like " interesting men."

March 9. I wonder, if my cough were to get very much worse, and I should go into consumption, whether Paul Brown would be a little sorry. I think the whole Browning Club would feel just a trifle sad. They would undoubtedly erect a beautiful marble monument over my grave, with the inscription: —

> "Fretless and free, soul, clap thy pinion,
> Earth have dominion, body, o'er thee."

There is a little poem of Browning's that persistently haunts me. This verse keeps running in my head: —

> "Was it something said,
>   Something done,
> Vexed him? was it touch of hand,
>   Turn of head?
> Strange! that very way
>   Love begun.
> I as little understand love's decay."

March 25. I cannot stand this sort of thing any longer. I am going to aunt Ruth's to make a visit. Is it possible that Paul felt as I do, when he used those same words, and I laughed at him?

I told them at the club that I should be absent from five meetings, and every one seemed to be very sorry except Mr. Brown. After the class was over, he said coldly that he regretted to hear that I was going away, for he should probably leave Northbridge before my return.

March 26. I did not know that the cocks crowed at such an unearthly hour.

They begin at three o'clock, and keep it up steadily until daylight. There are only three hours in the night when there is absolute silence. I never stayed awake all night before.

I am glad that I was so frigid and icy to Mr. Brown yesterday, so that he will never suspect how much I care, for I do care, — there is no use in trying to disguise the fact from myself. What a fool I have been!

March 30. That very afternoon, as I was sitting by the window, who should drive up to the door but Paul Brown! He had a little colloquy with mamma, who was just going out of the house; and she came back and told me to put on my fur-lined circular, as it would be so cold in driving, — as if it were a matter of course that I should drive about the country with Paul, when I have never done such a thing in my life. I opened the window.

"I am very busy," I said, "and I don't see how I can go."

"What are you so busy about?" he asked.

A BROWNING COURTSHIP

I held up a doll's dress that I was making for little Ruth.

"It is of the utmost importance that I should finish this garment to take away with me," I said gravely.

"Won't you come?" he asked beseechingly. "I may not see you for such a very long time."

Of course I "came." I had in fact meant to come, all along. He said nothing at first, and then he began to quote softly to himself from "The Last Ride Together:"—

> "'Take back the hope you gave—I claim
> Only a memory of the same,
> And this beside, if you will not blame,
> Your leave for one more last ride with me.'"

"Drive," I corrected, as flippantly as I could; but my heart was heavy with a foreboding that he considered everything at an end between us.

He did not quote any more, and for some time we talked on indifferent subjects. At last he said: "I wanted to see you this once, Miss Cheney, to tell you of my plans, and how I happen to be leaving Northbridge in this sudden fashion. I have had a good business opening offered me in Texas " —

" In Texas ! " I exclaimed involuntarily.

" Yes. Under the circumstances, I prefer to make an entire change, and I expect to start in a week."

I had a choking sensation, and felt the tears coming to my eyes. I never was in such physical misery in my life. I was determined that my face should show nothing, and so I resolutely drove back the tears, all but a little one, which might have passed for a raindrop ; for, as if in sympathy with the general dreariness, it was beginning to rain. I said nothing. I could not speak. At last Paul broke the silence.

" I wanted to say good-by to you alone, and not in the presence of Miss Niles and her phalanx," he said, with the suggestion of a smile.

" Good-by is a very little word ; it does not take long to say it," I observed, as carelessly as I could. " Do you mean that you are never coming back ? "

I tried so hard not to show what I felt

that I could hear my own words sounding strangely cold and formal, and as if it were a matter of entire indifference to me whether he came back or not.

"Yes, that is what I mean," he answered.

Then a sudden sense of desolation swept over me. I turned my face and looked at the big raindrops. The strain had been too much for me, and I began to shiver and tremble like an aspen leaf.

"Are you cold?" Paul asked. "You ought to have worn that fur-lined circular," and taking off his overcoat he enveloped me in it.

"Will he have no mercy?" I thought; for his kindness was harder to bear than his coldness had been.

"Yes, I am cold," I replied. "You yourself have told me so. Please take me home."

We had come to a dreary stretch through the leafless woods, and the desolate picture was completed by pools of dark water on either side of the road, and mounds of smirched and water-soaked snow.

"There is just one thing more that I want to say to you," Paul began. "I am going away; you know very well why. Well, there is nothing more to be said, only — only that I have loved you, and cannot help loving you." These words he uttered in quite a matter-of-fact tone. "I did not mean to tell you this when I brought you here," he continued abruptly, after a moment's pause. "I meant merely to bid you good-by. I have always vowed that I would never annoy a woman in this way but once, and — Why, May, dear May!"

I was crying. I could not help it. The tears that I had struggled against before came now, at the first suggestion of happiness, in an overwhelming, uncontrollable rush.

... I am very, very happy. Too happy to write, too happy to eat, too happy to sleep. As might have been expected, Miss Niles saw us driving back, and we looked so radiant that she spread the news of our engagement at once. So all Northbridge knows it, and they all say they are not surprised, which isn't possible, and all are pleased except Miss Anderson. It is a pleasure to make so many people happy.

May 5. My bliss would be complete if it were not for one little black cloud. Paul himself is so sincere that he will never be able to understand how I could pretend to care for Browning when I did not. I ought to confess the whole thing, but I have not the moral courage. If I could deceive him on such a vital point, won't he naturally conclude that I may deceive him in everything? Still, I am not wholly insincere, for I do want to like what he likes.

When Paul and I are driving, or walking, or sitting together, suddenly this apparition of Browning will pop up in my mind like a Jack-in-the-box. How easy it ought to be to make a confession! It could be done in five words, — "I do not like Browning;" or even in three, — "I detest Browning." Then I try to say this sentence aloud, but when I picture the pained look on Paul's face I have not the strength to utter it. I stay awake at night constructing little scenes, in which he is angry and grieved at first, but always forgiving in the end. I must be in a very nervous condition, or I should not make a serious matter out of such a trifle. But is it a trifle? I have let Paul think that I share his greatest enthusiasm. He still believes a love of Browning to be the strongest bond of sympathy between us. Then, in addition, I am haunted by the thought that if I had not been such a hypocrite he might have cared for Annie, in spite of her twenty-seven years, for she really loves Browning. The full enormity of my transgression never came to me until now.

"I detest Browning," — nothing easier to say in theory, nothing more difficult in practice.

May 20. I have spent such a wakeful night! Yesterday, at last, I screwed up my courage to speak of my secret. It was one of the first warm days, and we were in the orchard. Paul had taken out my little sewing-chair for me, and we sat under the apple blossoms, which every gust of wind sent in a pink shower all over my hair and my pale blue gown.

A BROWNING COURTSHIP

Paul was very happy, and unusually pleased with me.

"Yes, I will be brave and tell him," I resolved.

But just then he began to quote: —

"'Hark, where my blossomed pear-tree in the hedge
Leans to the field, and scatters on the clover
Blossoms and dew-drops at the bent spray's edge.'"

"I cannot tell him now," I thought. He had thrown himself on the grass by my side, and was lazily watching me with half-closed eyes, as I drew my needle swiftly in and out of my work.

I don't remember just how it began, but somehow or other he chose to talk of affectation, and how much he disliked it, and what a comfort it was that I was so absolutely genuine, so simple, and so unlike other women. I felt the color stealing into my cheeks at this undeserved praise.

"Paul," I began pleadingly, "suppose — suppose that you found that I was *not* as genuine as I seemed; suppose — suppose, in fact, that I were so *like* other women: would you still care for me, do you think?"

"I don't know," he answered, fixing his eyes on me with such an expression of love and confidence that I felt at once triumphant and humbled. "Why should we talk of what does not concern us? You are what you are, the sweetest, the truest" —

"But, Paul," I persisted, "I am really a different person from what you think, not as good, not as simple. There is a secret that I could tell you; and yet I am afraid, for *you* are so *absolutely* truthful, so thoroughly honest" —

"I! — good heavens!"

"Paul, what do you mean?" I cried, frightened by his tones.

"Nothing," he returned, vainly trying to reassure me, — "only you cannot have the monopoly of secrets. I too have one."

But alas! at this critical moment Miss Niles, in her green sunbonnet, indiscreetly came through the gap in the hedge, and, settling herself in the hammock, began to ask one question after another about Browning, and quoted him until she drove me into the house. For a thoroughly kind woman, Miss Niles is the most inconsiderate person I know.

I have not seen Paul alone since, and I stayed awake half the night torturing myself with theories about his secret.

May 21. Paul and I took a long drive this afternoon,— it is the only way in which we are sure to be free from interruptions,— and I tried unsuccessfully to worm his secret out of him.

"Paul," I began, "I think I know what it is that you are concealing from me. I feel sure that you have been in love with some charming but insincere girl, and are afraid to confess it to me. But that will make no difference; it won't trouble me if you have loved twenty girls, if only you care last and most for me."

Paul laughed softly to himself.

"You can set your mind at ease upon that point," he said. "My secret is something quite different. It has nothing to do with any woman."

"Has it to do with a man?" I inquired.

"Yes, it has to do with a man."

"I suppose it is some money difficulty,"

I suggested. "Dearest, I beg you to tell me all about it."

"No," said Paul, "it is nothing of that sort; it is not anything that will affect your happiness, if you do not know it. It will only make life a little harder for me, which is a just retribution. Do not think of it again. I ought never to have mentioned it."

It is very mysterious. However, I mean to put it out of my head, and go on as if nothing had happened; but if Paul will not tell me his secret, he certainly shall not learn mine; that is quite fair.

July 1. Uncle John, bless him, has decided to go abroad in the autumn for a year, and so Paul is to take all his practice, or clients, or whatever the proper term is. I shall have to study up legal phrases now, and there is a dear little house to be rented, just big enough for two people to begin housekeeping in. So we are to be married in November. I suppose we shall furnish our house chiefly with our wedding presents, for it is so many years since there has been a wedding among the *élite* of Northbridge that I am sure everybody will give us nice things.

October 2. Our presents have begun to flow in. There are two boxes waiting in the hall now, because I won't open them until Paul comes. One is from Mrs. Jansen, and I think it contains a silver tea-service, like the one she gave Lucy Fuller, because years ago she jokingly promised me one.

Evening. We have unpacked Mrs. Jansen's box. I saw almost immediately that it was full of books, exquisitely bound in white vellum. "Probably a set of Shakespeare," I thought; "they will be a great ornament to the book-case." I took up one volume, and found to my horror that the title was "The Red Cotton Night-Cap Country."

"Paul," I gasped, "it is a set of Browning, almost exactly like the one you gave me. Don't you suppose we can exchange Mrs. Jansen's present for silver?"

Paul opened one of the books, and found my name inscribed on the fly-leaf;

and alas! each volume had an appropriate quotation written in it, in Mrs. Jansen's exquisitely neat hand.

The other present was from Grace.

"This will be something worth having," I thought, as I eagerly opened it. It contained "Colombe's Birthday," illustrated with sketches that she made herself, the dear girl. It is lovely to have it, only — I wish I liked Browning better. Paul is very much pleased. He has a soul above spoons, and forks, and teapots.

October 5. It is very provoking. The whole Browning Class have run riot on the subject of their master, and each member has vied with the others in trying to find a delicate and original expression of her regard.

Miss Niles has had a picture painted on purpose for us, by a New York artist of sixth-rate ability. The subject is a scene from "In a Balcony." Constance and Norbert, in purple and green costumes, stand haranguing each other, and exchanging most sentimental glances; while just behind them is the queen in funereal black, stiff, stern, and implacable. The motto is, "I love once, as I live but once."

Dear Miss Niles! her intentions were good, but it is such a hideous picture that we shall have to banish it to the spare-room.

Miss Anderson has given us two of her Old Pictures in Florence, handsomely framed. I am glad Paul likes them so much. *I* think them hideous. They are photographs taken from the original paintings, and show all the imperfections. I can't see any beauty in a Madonna with a crack directly across her eyes, as if she wore spectacles. However, I bear up for Paul's sake. I am careful not to let him suspect my disappointment.

October 13. Colonel Parminter is a trump. He has sent us a huge square box. It is too big to contain Browning's works, and besides, I have taken pains to show Mrs. Jansen's edition to every one. Dear old Colonel Parminter! I begin to feel very remorseful for ever having made fun of him.

October 14. When Paul came he opened the box for me, while I stood by, indulging in speculations concerning the delightful contents.

"Do you know, Paul, I think it is one of those beautiful bronze lamps like Mrs. Ellis's!" I exclaimed eagerly, having caught a glimpse of something bronze.

"It is too heavy for a lamp," he returned. "I think it is — Why, it's a bust!" and pushing away the excelsior, he raised it on end, and the countenance gazed at me with a genial, kindly expression, and yet with a merry twinkle in the eye, as much as to say, "Well, my dear young lady, how do you feel now?"

It is needless to add that it was a life-sized bust of Robert Browning. I could have cried with vexation, if Paul had not been there.

I have gone back to my former opinion of Colonel Parminter.

October 20. It is the same old story repeated in different forms. Even the beautiful clock that Annie Fairchild has given us has a Browning motto engraved upon it: —

"Time's wheel runs back or stops,
Potter and clay endure."

A BROWNING COURTSHIP

Time's wheel won't stop long enough for me to tell of all the ingenious devices the club have resorted to, to vary their gifts, and yet have them connected with R. B.

Little Miss Perkins is the only member who has given me a wholly commonplace present. She handed me some silver sugar-tongs, with a somewhat abject air. "My dear," she said, "you know how I dislike Browning. I felt it would be an affectation in me to give you a present associated with him, so I've brought these sugar-tongs, and I hope you won't mind very much." I embraced her on the spot. The tongs are lovely, and just what I wanted.

October 25. It seems that Mrs. Ellis is going to send us a china tea-set. So "there is some light on the dark river."

October 26. The tea-set has come, and each cup and saucer has a Browning quotation around the edge! The way of the transgressor is hard!

We have just received a huge box from Paul's brother in England. I am very much excited about it, for as his brother

Philip is the rich member of the family, it is undoubtedly something delightful. . . .

My curiosity was so great that I could not possibly wait until Paul came, so Bridget and I together managed to open the box. I saw the present was something marble, and fancied all sorts of things. In another moment I discovered that it was merely a bust. This was disappointing, as I have never been fond of busts; but I rather like the head of Clytie, and hoped it might be that.

Bridget, with great difficulty, raised it and set it on the floor.

"Shure and it looks enough like that other gintleman to be his twin brother," she said, "barring that one is as black as the ace of spades, and the other white as the driven snow."

I looked at it with a sickening feeling at my heart. It was (there was no mistake about it; by this time the master's features were well imprinted upon my mind), — it was — a bust of Robert Browning!

I had been trying on gowns all day and was tired out; so as soon as Bridget had left the room, I threw myself down on the floor, and, leaning against R. B. for support, I wept bitterly. I laid my head against his marble head, and my tears coursed down his face. They might have melted a heart of stone, but produced no impression upon the unsympathetic countenance of Robert Browning.

Presently I heard a distressed voice say, "Why, May, darling, what is the matter?"

I sprang up and faced Paul. The hour had come, and I no longer faltered.

"*That* is the matter," I said, with the gesture of a tragedy queen. "Look at your brother's present."

"But I do not understand," Paul said, bewildered. "I thought you could not have too much Browning."

"I have never liked Browning, never from the first moment that I saw you, never through all these long months."

I did not dare to look at Paul to see how he bore this announcement, but I heard him exclaim under his breath, "Is it possible!"

"Yes," I said, "it is, unfortunately,

too true. I have been a hypocrite, and willfully deceived you. You know my secret now. Break our engagement, if you choose. Whatever happens, I can endure this life of deceit no longer. I shall die of too much Browning."

I was terribly excited, and flung myself, trembling, on the sofa.

In a moment Paul was at my side. "Dearest May" — he entreated.

I pushed his hand away.

"I am not worthy to touch you," I cried, — "you who care so much for Browning; you who" —

"May," said Paul contritely, "I once told you that I had concealed something from you. I also have had 'too much Browning:' that is my secret." . . .

October 27. This morning a note came from Paul's brother Philip for me. I will copy it here: —

MY DEAR NEW SISTER, — I am delighted to learn, through Paul, that you are as great an admirer of Browning as I am myself. I am glad, also, to hear that you have been a sufficiently powerful advocate to convert him. He used to be only a half-hearted admirer, in the old days, but he tells me that he has been thriving on my reputation, and conducting a Browning Class for your sweet sake. I have been trying to think what I could give you for a wedding present that you will not have a score of already, and I have decided to send you a bust of Browning, to put as a genial household god above your hearthstone.

Your affectionate brother,

PHILIP KENT BROWN.

I looked at Paul, and he looked at me, and then we both laughed.

"I can't get over my surprise that *you* should carry on this long course of deceit," I observed.

"Really, I was not so much to blame as you think," he said, "for I told Miss Niles squarely, in the beginning, that it was my brother who was the distinguished P. K. Brown. I did not mean to join the class at first, but after I had seen you — well, it was all over with me then, for I fell in love with you at first sight. I felt it was my best chance of pleasing you," he added, with a smile; "and I liked Browning well enough to begin with, but Miss Niles and the colonel were too many for me."

"Paul," I said pensively, after a moment given to retrospection, "we can never tell our kind friends what hypocrites we have been; it would give them too much pain. We shall have to bear the consequences of our deceit for all time. Do you know that even our wedding is to be different from other people's? Miss Niles revealed to me, in a burst of confidence, that the organist is to play, what do you suppose, as we come out of church? A Toccata, by Galuppi! Miss Niles says she hopes that we shall march through life to Browning music."

"Heaven forbid!" said Paul.

COMMONPLACE CARRIE

I

THE spring sunshine was coming in at the west window of Professor Bainbridge's room, and making a painful glare across the papers which were scattered on the table that was drawn up to the slippery horsehair sofa upon which he was lying. The room was ugly and commonplace, and the professor had an insuperable objection to both of these characteristics. He sighed as he glanced at the impossible brick-colored roses with arsenic-green leaves, that formed the pattern of the wall-paper, which, to make it still more unendurable, was divided into diamond-shaped compartments by heavy black lines supposed to indicate a lattice. There were six roses and three buds in each diamond; how many times he had counted them! The walls were adorned with uninteresting engravings and portraits of the class that are banished to the attic in houses where respect for art outweighs respect for family. The professor sighed once more when he thought of the dreary weeks that he must pass in these uncongenial surroundings. But at this point his attention was arrested by the sound of voices in the porch below him; one was the familiar treble of the daughter of the house, while the other was that of an elderly neighbor.

"Do tell me something about your new boarder, Professor Bainbridge," she was asking. "Hannah Harwood says that he has written learned books and clever short stories that have made a great stir. Is that a fact?"

Fame is sweet, no matter from how humble a source it is awarded. The professor smiled complacently.

"Mr. Bainbridge is a professor at a Western college," the younger voice answered indifferently, "and I believe he has written some stories."

"So Hannah was right," Mrs. Brown responded. "I thought she must be mistaken, for I caught a glimpse of him the day he came to town as he drove past our house, and I thought he looked *very* insignificant."

At this juncture, the professor began to be troubled by doubts as to whether he ought to listen to a conversation which evidently had not been designed for his amusement.

"What's the matter with him?" inquired Mrs. Brown.

"He has overworked, and had a low, nervous fever, which has left him — out of spirits, to put it mildly. You know he came here to be under Uncle Frank's care, but the Sanitarium is full, so we have taken him in."

"What does he say and do? Tell me everything; it is *so* interesting to hear about nervous patients."

"He doesn't say anything; that is just the trouble," Carrie Swift replied. "He sat perfectly silent at table for the first four days after he came, when, to the relief of the family, he took to his room with water on the knee."

"The poor man must have melancholia. Does he literally never speak?"

"He can talk enough to ask for fifty things he wants, and to send me up and down stairs twenty times a day to get them, but not enough to be polite. I don't see any excuse for his looking like a funeral; I believe people can be cheerful if they choose; but Uncle Frank says"— here the speaker's voice was lowered, and the professor became doubly sure that it was dishonorable to listen any longer. He tortured himself with vain speculations as to the revelations that followed, which he knew only too well must be inimical to himself. The thoughts thus suggested followed him into the night, and banished sleep effectually from his eyelids.

The next morning he awaited Miss Swift's arrival with feverish impatience. She came at last, bringing him his breakfast, as usual.

"I hope you had a good night," she said, as she deposited the tray on the table by his side.

"Thank you, I did not sleep at all," he replied coldly.

Carrie Swift gave him a glance at once

compassionate and contemptuous. She was a little creature, with a slight, undeveloped figure, and a careworn expression that seemed unsuited to her nineteen years.

"Sit down," said the professor in a peremptory tone. "There is something that I wish to say to you."

Carrie obeyed.

"I could not help overhearing a part of your conversation with your friend last evening," he went on swiftly, "and I regret exceedingly to have given you so much trouble. I beg you to believe that I shall be more considerate in future; but in return I will request you to abstain from talking me over."

His manner was haughty, even stern, for there was nothing about the sharp-featured, freckled young person before him to arouse either his interest or consideration. He thought her face one of the plainest that he had ever seen, and its lack of physical attraction was not atoned for by any charm of expression.

As she listened to his words a painful flush mounted to her cheeks. "I — I —

am sorry that you heard me," she stammered.

"I am glad that, as such observations were made, I overheard them."

"After all," and she faced him with a look half appealing, half defiant, "it was the truth."

"Did that justify you in gossiping about me? Put yourself in my place. Imagine yourself confined to your room, with your nervous system in a shattered condition, and little occupation but your morbid fancies, and ask yourself if, under these conditions, it would be easy to retain your cheerfulness? If you became depressed and silent, would you enjoy being held up for ridicule to the whole neighborhood?" Professor Bainbridge had grown angry under the recapitulation of his wrongs. "Will you promise to desist from discussing me in future?" he concluded in an authoritative and superior tone that roused his companion, who would gladly have agreed to anything had he been more considerate.

"I will promise nothing," she said, with a flash from her gray eyes. "Do you think you have a harder time than the rest of us? Put yourself in my place. Imagine yourself washing dishes and sweeping rooms until you were ready to drop, and having to stay at home from drives and sewing-circles in the afternoon because somebody might want to have the window open, and then find that there was a draught and want it shut again. Somebody who never spoke to you except to say 'thank you,' shortly, as if he thought he should die if he said anything more. Do you suppose *I* find it easy to be cheerful? And yet I manage it."

Greatly to Carrie's surprise, the professor laughed softly.

"Poor girl, you do have a hard time," he said pleasantly. "Suppose we each try to do what we can toward the amelioration of the conditions of the other?"

His genial manner recalled her to herself.

"Oh, what have I said!" she exclaimed ruefully. "How rude I have been to talk in this way to you, who are a professor, and so old! Please forgive me. Ethel is always telling me that I must not say whatever comes into my head, without stopping to think. Ethel Sanford is my most intimate friend. She used to live in Longfield. Ethel is not a bit like me. She is lovely to everybody, even to Mrs. Brown, whom she hates. I will never say another word to Mrs. Brown about you, although it will be hard, for she asks so many questions. It must be dreadful to be shut up in one's room all day. When you have had your breakfast, and I have done the housework, perhaps there is something that I could do to amuse you?"

"Would you read to me?" he asked eagerly.

"Yes. Mother says that I read awfully, but as she has a cold I will do the best I can."

Mr. Bainbridge awaited her return with actual impatience. Her flash of anger had done what her fortnight of patient toil on his behalf had failed to do. It had given him an interest in the study of her character. To be sure, it was not of a type that would have attracted him under other circumstances; but the inveterate student of character is grateful for the slightest indication of variety where he has expected monotony.

It was late in the afternoon before Carrie was able to comply with her promise. She found the professor with an open book by his side.

"It seems, Miss Carrie, that I am to be followed by one misfortune after another for the rest of my life," he said testily. "After cutting me down to using my eyes only one hour a day, your uncle has now forbidden my using them at all. If I am to be lame and blind, I might far better have given up my existence when I had my fever."

Patience had not been one of Professor Bainbridge's most conspicuous virtues in the days of his prosperity, but in his adversity it deserted him entirely, as the long-suffering Carrie discovered in the weeks which followed. He, on his side, found that Mrs. Swift had but a too well-grounded opinion of her daughter's elocutionary powers. His patience was sorely tried by the way in which she spoiled the rhythm of poetry; but on the other hand, her views concerning novels were an unfailing source of entertainment to him. He amused himself by trying a series of experiments in the course of which he and his young friend wandered in a somewhat vagrant manner through the fields of English literature.

One afternoon Mr. Bainbridge handed "Sartor Resartus" to Carrie. "Will you be so kind as to read me this chapter on 'The Everlasting Yea'?" he asked. "I like to read it when I wish to put myself into 'good tune,' if I may be allowed the expression. Carlyle always raises one's groveling spirit to a higher mood."

It gave him great pleasure to say things of this kind to Miss Swift.

She took the book and began to read, stumbling over the unfamiliar words, and treating her auditor to a running commentary on the text. After half an hour spent in this way she laid down the volume and said:—

"What queer stuff. What is it all about, any way?"

The professor gave her a brief account of Teufelsdröckh's life. "He was an unhappy man," he said in conclusion. "Like the rest of us he was fighting his way through doubt to truth, through temptation and suffering to more abundant life. 'Name it as we choose,' he quoted, ' with or without visible devil; whether in the natural desert of rocks and sands, or in the populous moral desert of selfishness and baseness, to such temptation are we all called.' Do you feel as if you were in a moral desert of selfishness and baseness, Miss Carrie?" he inquired, with the half-amused, half-kindly smile that she had grown to know so well.

"Sometimes, when you are cross with me because your knee does n't improve any faster."

"What a base slanderer you are! Go on, please."

She obeyed, and read without comment until she reached the end of the following sentence: "Beautiful it was to sit there, as in my skyey tent, musing and meditating; on the high table-land, in front of the mountains; over me, as roof, the azure dome, and around me, for walls, four azure, flowing curtains, — namely, the four azure winds, on whose bottom fringes also I have seen gilding."

At this point Carrie looked up from her book. "I hope the poor man had his overcoat on, and a shawl too," she observed; "for if he was blown upon by all four winds at once he would need to be well wrapped up, especially as he seems to have been a sickly individual."

"You wretch!" the professor exclaimed, trying not to yield to his desire to laugh. "Have you no soul? You have spoiled one of the most beautiful passages in the English language for me. I can never read it again without fancying Herr Teufelsdröckh wrapped up in a blanket shawl."

"But he didn't wear one, so don't disturb yourself; he was just the kind of man to be imprudent, and he hadn't Uncle Frank, and mother, and me to look after him."

"No, poor fellow!"

Carrie began to read again, and her criticisms continued in the same vein.

"Oceans of Hockheimer," she said at last. "A throat like Op — some kind of a cuss; you can pronounce that word, Mr. Bainbridge."

"Ophiuchus."

"Thank you. 'Speak not of them.' (I am sure that is the last thing *I* want to do.) 'To the infinite shoeblack they are as nothing!' Well, that shoeblack is the only sensible person I've come across."

"Look here," cried the professor, losing all patience, and snatching the volume from her. "You shall not murder Carlyle any longer."

"I suppose this is the 'higher mood' that you wanted him to get you into," she said, as she rose to leave the room.

"Don't go; stay and talk to me, or let me teach you chess; you promised that I might some day."

"I've got to clear out a closet this afternoon, and do heaps of sewing on the machine, and trim a hat for Fanny, and I ought to make some calls."

The professor reflected for a moment. "What a useful life you lead," he remarked at last. "I don't know what this family would do without you."

"One expects to be useful in one's family."

"You do, at all events. Does it not bring a sense of thorough satisfaction to be so indispensable?"

"I never thought about it."

"You rarely occupy your mind with yourself, I fancy."

"What's the use," she said briskly, "when everything else is so much more interesting?"

This remark evidently opened a wide field of speculation to the professor, for he meditated upon it for some time in silence. At last Carrie renewed her attempt to go.

"When you are alone, what do you think about?" Mr. Bainbridge asked, as she stood opposite him with her hand on the door-knob.

"That depends upon the time of day; early in the morning I think about housework, and the rest of the time I divide my thoughts between you and mother, and the sewing-machine, until evening, when I think of my small sisters; it is strange, but I think of them regularly every night at eight o'clock."

"You enviably busy creature! But when your work is over, how do you occupy your mind then?"

"When my work is over, I go to sleep."

"Happy girl! I wish I could go to sleep with such ease. When you chance to lie awake, however, do you never worry over your shortcomings? are you never beset by the cruel problems of life?"

"No; I wish I had n't taken a cup of coffee. That is always my first and last thought when I lie awake at night."

Certainly this young girl was amusing; so much the professor conceded as she glanced back at him mischievously when she left the room. He was growing to have a kindly feeling for her, apart from his interest in her as a study. Her unconsciousness and simplicity pleased him, and she piqued his curiosity.

At length he grew bold enough to give her a short tale of his own to read. The scene was laid in Florence five centuries ago, and the little romance had attracted far more attention than his "Historical Sketches," which covered the same period. He was aware that the story had received greater praise than it deserved, and he was anxious to learn the opinion of an unprejudiced mind which would be alike unaffected by fashion and regard for himself.

When Carrie finished reading "A Mosaic of the Thirteenth Century," she gave it to her mother to return to the professor, a circumstance which that observant man did not fail to note.

He would not let Miss Swift off thus easily. The next time he saw her, he demanded her opinion. "How do you like my romance?" he inquired.

"Since you ask me, I am sorry"— she began, then hesitated.

"Don't be afraid to say just what you think."

"Well, then, *I hate* it."

"Thank you; most people who find the plot and characters disagreeable, praise the local color, and what they term 'the atmosphere of the thirteenth century.'"

"I never lived in the thirteenth century, so I don't know anything about its atmosphere."

"Do you think my sketch artistic?" he asked, with his accustomed smile.

"I suppose so," she said doubtfully. "All the disagreeable stories that Ethel admires are artistic, she says. I never know whether books are artistic or not"—and she raised her eyes with a childlike candor that ought to have disarmed her tormentor.

"You take no pleasure then in art, apart from subject, nor in form and color?" he went on. "You have, I fear, no æsthestic taste."

Her face grew crimson. If he chose to amuse himself at her expense she need not spare him.

"I *hate* your story from beginning to end," she said with a certain fierceness. "I can't see what good there is in writing about such horrid things and wicked people. I should be ashamed to have such ideas come into my head. I don't wonder you had nervous prostration afterwards."

The professor lay back on the sofa and laughed heartily, notwithstanding that Carrie looked perturbed as she left the room.

It was late in the afternoon when Mr. Bainbridge next saw her. He had been expecting her for some time before he heard her business-like knock on the door. She came in, bringing him his tea on an ugly black waiter adorned by a gilt landscape that had been dimmed by age; the china which held his repast was brown and white, and Carrie wore a blue and white checked apron over a dark green dress.

"Here is a case illustrating my point," said the professor, reverting to the subject of their former interview. "Had you any of the æsthetic passion, you would have put on your pretty white apron, and brought me my tea in those Faience dishes on the red waiter, in which case you would have made a harmonious picture."

The poor child was tired and out of spirits, and this was a little too much to bear in silence. "I guess you would n't have any time to think about the æsthetic passion if you were as busy as I am," she returned, " or to stop and think what colors looked best together." She rushed out of the room to hide her tears. When the professor next saw her her eyelids were red and swollen.

"My dear Miss Carrie," he said penitently, " I have been both rude and ungrateful to my faithful little nurse, who is so much better to a crusty old fellow than he deserves. Will you forgive me ?" and he held out his hand with a pleading motion. Carrie did not take it. She looked at him wearily. His face had grown unusually gentle.

" It isn't so much that I am angry at what you have said," she explained, in a burst of confidence. "It is that sometimes I feel as if I never did anything to suit anybody, and then I get cross and hate myself. I can't ever make a pretty picture, because I am so hideous. I wish Ethel were here ; perhaps she may come for a visit before you go ; she is lovely, and has such pretty clothes ; but after all, it isn't my fault that I am plain and stupid, and can't find time to make any more white aprons."

The professor gave one of his provoking laughs, but instantly grew grave. The pathos of the girl's life had suddenly and powerfully appealed to his sympathies. How young she was to have so much care! He saw the dull years stretching on for her in endless succession, filled with humdrum duties, and unillumined by any of the light which an imaginative person throws around the future, to make the dreary present more endurable. The unselfishness of her character struck him as it had never done before.

"Come," he said, in his most persuasive manner, "you have not forgiven me yet; pray do, and let us be better friends in the future."

"I don't know that I want to be better friends. The more you knew me, the more you would laugh at me. I don't believe you ever like people for themselves alone. I will take your waiter now, please," — and she held out her hand for it.

He took her hand and clasped it firmly in his. "You do me an injustice," he said. "I like you now for yourself alone, and I want you to like me for myself alone, and not because I have some reputation as an author, or" —

"I certainly shall not like you on account of your books," she interrupted playfully. She was almost charming when her face lighted up in that unexpected way. The professor still kept her hand. "Will you forgive me?" he reiterated.

"I will forgive you, but we are not the kind to be friends."

"You mean we are not '*sympatica*,' as the Italians say; but that is not necessary."

"If Ethel were only here!" — and she gently withdrew her hand; "she is intellectual and sympathetic, and" —

"I am thankful she is not here," he broke in impatiently. It piqued him to have his unusual advances met with such indifference. "I am sorry that you dislike me," he added coldly.

"How foolish you are! I don't dislike you, but there is a long way between not disliking a person and wishing to be friends with him. How I hate all this talk about one's feelings," she said vehemently. She had risen and was standing opposite the window, and her face suddenly became radiant.

"Uncle Frank has come back from Boston," she announced in great excitement. She left the room precipitately, and presently the professor saw her run down the street and greet her uncle with outstretched arms. "She is a good lover," he reflected; "how she would worship a husband!" No man with a spark of sentiment or imagination could fall in love with her, he told himself, but her friendship would be something worth having.

For those of us who remain in this world, spring always ends in summer, ultimately, no matter how lengthened the process may be. It was greatly protracted in Longfield, not only from climatic causes, but likewise for internal and domestic reasons. It seemed to Professor Bainbridge, who had never before experienced a New England spring, as if house-cleaning were the chief event of the season, and the delicious carols of the thrushes and catbirds, the dim, feathery sheen of the opening leaves, and the fields starred with anemones or dotted with dandelions were so many impertinent interruptions to the one important business in life. He was well enough to take long drives into the country with Carrie's uncle, the doctor, and sometimes she herself was his companion; but her mind on these occasions was apt to revert to the best method for killing moths, or to an infallible means of exterminating Buffalo beetles. In spite of her limitations, however, his friendship with Carrie grew as the weeks passed. When summer at last took the place of spring, its advent was marked by unusual festivity in the little town. The professor concluded that the industrious housewives were eager to exhibit the fruits of their labors, for they gave a series of tea-drinkings in their immaculate houses, at which all their best china figured, as well as the new gowns which had been as important a feature in the spring of the younger portion of the community, as the sweeping and garnishing of their dwellings had been with their elders.

The professor was not a social man; or

rather, to be accurate, he never thought it worth his while to be civil to persons who bored him, and the society in Longfield was such as to elicit nothing but monosyllables from him. Genius has this privilege, — it may be rude without losing any of its prestige; and whatever his reputation might be in the world at large, in Longfield Professor Bainbridge stood for Genius (spelled with a capital G).

Carrie, who knew how delightful the professor could be when he chose, was not satisfied with his behavior when in company. One evening she took him to task.

"If you go to the Petersons' lawn party to-morrow," she said, "you must be just as agreeable as you can; of course you don't find Longfield people pleasant when you are disagreeable to them."

"I consider it a breach of truthfulness to appear to like persons whom I in reality detest," Mr. Bainbridge returned, with the air of supporting a valuable moral principle.

"Really," Carrie said, throwing back her head, and putting all the sarcasm of which she was capable into her voice. "When Fanny does as you do, we say she is a very naughty little girl. That is just the difference between a little girl and a great man," she mused, "a really famous man. Mrs. Peterson asked me the other day if I did not feel it a privilege to be under the same roof with so much greatness. At first I thought she meant the new parlor curtains."

"'Greatness' feels contemptibly small this evening, Miss Carrie, so please don't take him down any more than is necessary."

"What is the matter?"

"I have a furious headache. The whole top of my head seems to be coming off." He flung himself down on the parlor sofa as he spoke. "I have no doubt I am in for another fever."

"Men always think they are on the brink of the grave when they have a headache," Carrie remarked. "Mother has one nearly every week, but she has never had a fever."

In spite of these unsympathetic words she was truly sorry for him. Suffering of body appealed to her as suffering of mind did not; it was something tangible and comprehensible: it was beyond the control of the patient, and within the province of the nurse.

"I can sometimes drive away mother's headaches by stroking her forehead," she said. "Perhaps I can cure you; may I try?"

"Indeed you may."

Carrie's touch was firm, yet gentle. It soothed the professor and carried him back, with a skip of thirty years, to the days of his childhood, when another hand with a motion as firm and gentle had put him to sleep night after night. He had been rather a pathetic little boy, with a tendency to sleeplessness even in those early days. He thought of his mother's premature death, and of his lonely life; while Carrie's hand traveled across his forehead, making a running accompaniment to his reveries.

"You must tell me if you do not like this," she said anxiously.

"I do like it; I cannot tell you how much good it is doing me."

The fine side of Carrie's nature appealed to him irresistibly. He was lost in admiration of her utter unconsciousness of self. She was trying to help him as simply and unaffectedly as if she were a sister of charity and he a hospital patient.

He forgot that he had ever been vexed by her lack of appreciation and that he had once thought her commonplace. He longed to seize her hand and tell her how great a blessing her friendship might be to him. He wanted to say that her strength and unconsciousness humbled him; but he judged rightly that at the first hint of these things her hand would be withdrawn and the growing peace of their intercourse troubled.

At length there was the sound of the opening of the long French window opposite them. The professor moved uneasily, while the color mounted to his face. Carrie remained undisturbed. She put up her hand with a warning gesture, as her mother, accompanied by the ubiquitous Mrs. Brown and her friend Miss Harwood, entered the room.

"Hush!" she said, "he is just going to sleep; he has a bad headache."

Mrs. Brown and Miss Harwood exchanged significant glances. The professor treacherously kept silent.

"Carrie," said Mrs. Swift gently, "will you please take my bonnet upstairs, and bring down my eyeglasses?"

II

The afternoon of Mrs. Peterson's lawn party was bright, but insufferably hot, a fortunate combination, as the weather enabled the guests to be present, and furnished them with an unfailing topic of conversation. Carrie and the professor arrived upon the scene in due season, and were instantly separated by Miss Harwood, who kept Mr. Bainbridge's eloquence to herself for half an hour, much to the regret of Kitty Peterson.

After a lengthy comparison between New England in the present day and Italy in the thirteenth century, Miss Harwood touched upon the women of both countries.

"You would not say what you do about the loss of beauty in New England if you could see Ethel Sandford," she said at last. "She is of the golden-haired Titian type, and a fascinating creature besides."

"Miss Sandford appears to be not only the most beautiful of her sex, but a paragon of all the virtues and intellectual graces also," the professor returned. "I confess I am tired of hearing Aristides called 'The Just.'"

"Still harping upon the great men of the thirteenth century?" asked Mrs. Peterson, who had caught the last clause of this sentence. "They were all giants, those men of that fertile period," she added in a tone of deep conviction, "but I myself don't think Aristides quite equal to Dante; Dante now seems to me a grand poet."

It was almost tea time before the professor could make his way to Carrie. "It is comfortable to get back to you," he said, sinking lazily on the bench by her side, with a sigh of relief. "I have been bored to death between discussions of the state of the weather and the state of Italy in the thirteenth century. Every one in Longfield has been studying up on the subject. People fancy that it is my one interest. I have returned to you for rest, after the incessant flow of witty and wise conversation."

"Because I am stupid and silent. Thank you."

"You are very perverse, and always will twist my compliments into reproaches. I mean that you are a most restful little person." He had some roses in his hand. "The prettiest Miss Peterson gave me these," he said, as he offered them to her; "do put them in your belt, they contrast so well with your blue dress."

"I can't take them; Kitty would n't like it."

"*I* cannot wear them," he said.

"You have no sentiment; when a young lady gives you flowers you must treasure them carefully, — at least until you are out of her sight."

"It is you who have no sentiment," observed her companion.

"I really must n't take them," Carrie

said, but there was a shade of doubt in her tone.

"Just these two, they will never be missed," he urged. Carrie succumbed with a thrill of pleasure, realizing for the first time what it was to be young and a woman. The professor smiled down upon her.

"This is enjoyment," said he. "What is needed to complete our perfect contentment?"

"A back to this seat, and cooler weather."

"You prosaic and ungrateful girl! Do you mean to say that the devotion of 'greatness' is not sufficient to make you forget these little drawbacks?"

"But you are not devoted to me; if you were you would fan me. Everybody fans Ethel, always."

The professor took her fleecy white fan. "It looks like a pile of snow-flakes," said he. "Is it swan's down?"

"No, it is made of goose-feathers. I pasted them all on cardboard myself. Don't you admire my ingenuity?"

"All my swans are your geese," he

murmured, as he slowly moved her fan back and forth.

"How little breeze you make! I'll show you how," — and she took possession of her fan. "There, see the difference," she added, as she briskly set the air in motion.

"You always do everything well; what will become of me when I no longer have my little friend to act as guide and caretaker? You cannot be so cruel as to say that we are not the 'kind' to be friends now?" he persisted. "I want you for my friend. At least we are better friends than we were at first?" he demanded, spurred on by her silence.

"I should hope so; at first you were detestable."

He joined in her laugh. "I wish this pleasant summer was not to end so soon," he proceeded. "I am sorry that I rashly promised to go to the Rangeley Lakes week after next; and in a month or two I shall be back in my dull routine in the West. I wish we lived nearer each other. I wish" — He stopped abruptly, for he had caught sight of a face and figure that he had never seen before. He was sure that the slender girl who was coming slowly toward them down the garden path was, like himself, a stranger in Longfield. She was not unusually pretty, but she was extremely graceful, and her white dress fitted her to perfection, and was a marvel of simplicity and taste. She wore a hat with rather a broad brim, and a wreath of pink sweetbrier around it. It threw a shadow over her face, and made the waves of golden-brown hair on her forehead seem remote and mysterious.

Carrie was waiting for the end of the professor's sentence. At last she looked up. "Ethel!" she cried in excitement. "My dear, when did you come? Kitty did n't tell me she expected you this week. You must come to us as soon as you can. How lovely, how altogether charming this is," and she flung her arms around her friend with utter disregard of spectators.

Mr. Bainbridge lingered in the vicinity, but it was some moments before Carrie remembered to present him to Ethel.

"I already know Miss Sandford well by reputation," he said after the introduction had been accomplished, "and I need not add that her reputation has not suffered at the hands of her friend."

Carrie moved away to help pass the salad, and Ethel took the half of the bench which she had left, while the professor dropped into his old seat. He was more animated than Carrie had ever seen him. "What a contrast to the way in which he talks to me," she thought, as she glanced at them from time to time. "There he goes to get her a comfortable chair, but I might have broken my back on that bench until the day of judgment and he would n't have done anything about it. He is fanning her, I knew he would, and he is doing it as if he had been used to it all his life, and with what an air of devotion! If a girl is plain and has n't any intellect, a man stops liking her just as soon as a pretty, bright girl appears, although instead of doing things for him, she makes him wait on her. It is n't very fair, but it 's natural; I should like a pretty girl better than a plain one if I were a man. He has taken the advice I gave him last evening," she thought with a little smile, in spite of her heartache; "for once he is making himself as agreeable as he can."

Some of the petals from one of her roses fell at her feet. She took them both out of her belt, and after looking at them regretfully she tore them to pieces. Her brief hour of triumph was over.

Love is often accused of blindness, but the most virulent detractors of the little god have never charged him with being lame. Friendship, on the contrary, is clearer sighted, but her approach is seldom swift. She stumbles on with many a halt, but her eyes are sharp, if her feet are clumsy; and when she has made sure that there are no more brambles and pitfalls in the way, she reaches her goal at last. Love, because of his blindness, takes no heed of obstructions, but rushes to his destination with feverish haste and outstrips the laggard friendship.

Mr. Bainbridge was in love; he had a friendly feeling for Carrie Swift, but he loved Ethel Sandford. He had known

Carrie intimately for the past three months, and he had talked for three hours with Ethel.

The week after the lawn party, Miss Sandford came to the Swifts' to make a visit. The professor had thought it impossible to cancel his engagement to go to the Rangeley Lakes, but he contrived to do it with apparent ease, and stayed on in Longfield.

One evening after Ethel had been for two or three weeks at the Swifts' house, the professor came back from a drive, — having left her and Mrs. Swift at the other end of the town, where they wanted to make a call, — to find Carrie sitting on the front porch with her knitting. He seated himself by her side, partly through remorse, for he had forgotten her existence of late, and partly for want of a better occupation.

"Have you had a pleasant drive?" she asked.

"Very," he said, with a sudden consciousness of how much greater the pleasure had been than when she was his companion.

"Whom did you see?" Carrie inquired.

"No one."

"And you actually went all the way to South Swanset without seeing a living soul?" she demanded playfully. "I suppose you were too much absorbed in philosophy to notice such trifles as people."

"We were absorbed in wondering who lived in the different houses, and what sort of lives they led," said the professor with asperity.

"If I had been there I could have told you," said Carrie. "What especial houses were you interested in?"

He described one.

"Abijah Patten, who used to be our butterman, has just moved there. Mother ought to have known that. His sister is a bony old maid of fifty, — I know I shall look like her some day, — and she is as sharp as vinegar, but she makes good butter. That is a nice old farmhouse, though; if we were very poor I wouldn't mind living there."

"Wouldn't you? Miss Sandford wondered how any one could endure life in such a lonely place."

"I could be happy anywhere with father and mother and the children, and work enough to keep me busy."

"I really believe you could," said the professor, with a smile. "You agree with me in thinking that place makes little difference in happiness. I could be happy anywhere with one or two chosen friends and plenty of books."

"Yes," she responded, "if you had a few cartloads of books and some one whose character you could study, I believe you would be happy at the north pole; only the person would have to be changed for a new one as soon as you had made out his character."

"You are unfair, Miss Carrie; whatever my attitude may be to the world at large, I am capable of strong attachments, as my friends can testify."

"I should like to see your friends," she mused. "One of them is the gentleman you have had so many letters from, I suppose?"

"Yes. The others are out of my reach

at present; one is in California, the other in Japan."

"Have n't you but three friends?"

"Not according to the best definition of the word. Are there so many persons for whom you would be willing to make any sacrifice, and whom you can depend upon in return, that you think three friends such a small number?"

"There is a great difference between being willing to do things for people, and having them ready to do things for you," she said slowly, bending her head over her knitting.

"In a perfect friendship each must be equally willing to help."

Carrie was silent; she wondered if, when the professor had asked her to be his friend, he had meant anything so great as this; but her common sense told her directly that he must have had in mind only the usual definition of the word, or he could not have forgotten that conversation. Why had Ethel come just as the professor had begun to be so kind? Ethel had such hosts of friends that one more or less could make little difference in her life. Carrie's eyes filled with tears as she reflected that there was not a person who would think of making any sacrifice for her outside of her own family circle, whereas there were many people for whom she would be willing to do the smallest thing, or the greatest, — and Mr. Bainbridge was among them. She thought that if she had planned the world she would have made the plain, uninteresting people without any heart, and then they would not have minded having no friends.

"Suppose we walk to the other end of the village to meet your mother and Miss Sandford?" suggested the professor.

Carrie was silent.

"Won't you come?" he persisted.

She shook her head and went quickly into the house; he followed her and the sound of a suppressed sob met his ear.

"Miss Carrie, what is the matter?" he asked stupidly.

"I have a bad headache, and am too tired to go to walk, so I will say goodnight."

He took her hand kindly, and said in

soothing tones : "You must take care of yourself or you will break down, and then what should we all do?"

Carrie snatched away her hand and impatiently turned to go upstairs.

"You must come to drive with us to-morrow night," he continued. "You shall sit on the front seat with me and point out all the people we meet, and give me their family histories, and tell me who lives in all the different houses."

This speech exasperated her past endurance. "You are very good," she said in an icy tone, "but has it never occurred to you that even *your* society may not satisfy every one at all times as completely as you think?"

She disappeared into the house, leaving Mr. Bainbridge deeply aggrieved; yet strange to say, what pained him most was the fear that she might be echoing Miss Sandford's sentiments, — for Carrie had been very friendly with him once. He asked himself why he should be thus cruelly pained at the thought that Miss Sandford did not like him; for it was not a new one, — he had often felt sure that she was merely amusing herself with him as she had done with a score of others. It is all very well to study character, but it is not so agreeable to encounter a fellow-student in that branch of sociology, who is bent upon remorselessly dissecting one's own traits. "I have no doubt that she makes the same satirical, lazy comments about me which she treats me to whenever her Longfield friends come up for discussion," he thought.

Spring had lingered in Longfield, but as if to make up for loss of time, summer departed with uncompromising swiftness. Autumn had come, and was flaunting its badges on every hillside and in all the valleys. The world was yellow and red and russet brown with the changing leaves. The little town was transformed, and every roadside, however insignificant, was a garden for a brief season. The fringed-gentian lifted its modest head and caught the hue of the sky, and the purple aster subdued the otherwise too brilliant coloring of the sumach bushes and the omnipresent goldenrod.

Mr. Bainbridge's departure came with

that of the summer; his last day had actually arrived.

Longfield, as it may be imagined, had been in a state of suspense throughout the past two months with regard to the professor's "intentions;" and on this evening as Mrs. Brown and Miss Harwood wended their way to Mrs. Swift's house, he was under discussion.

"The little heart he has," said Mrs. Brown, "is evidently at Ethel Sandford's disposal. If I were in his place I should marry Carrie Swift. Ethel is a very good sort of girl to be in love with, but for daily home comfort, give me honest, simple little Carrie."

"Mr. Bainbridge would be quite willing to let you have her, Sophie," Miss Harwood returned. "What would he do with a wife who could not sympathize with his intellectual tastes sufficiently to treat the thirteenth century with anything but levity?"

"A man has other tastes besides intellectual ones, and he cannot dine on the thirteenth century," Mrs. Brown retorted.

They had reached the Swifts' gate;

when they entered the house a moment later, they found the professor sitting with Ethel and Carrie in the front parlor. The girls were sewing, and he was reading aloud to them.

Mrs. Brown had come to beg clothes for a certain poor family for whose needs she had so much practical sympathy that the just professor was forced to admit that even she had her virtues. He was unreasonably angry with Ethel, however, for treating her with distinguished cordiality, when she had joined with him the moment before her entrance in an unsparing dissection of her faults.

Ethel was making some buttonholes in a pink cashmere waist, which she presently handed to Carrie, saying that she would accept her offer gratefully, as she hated to make buttonholes.

"It is convenient to have a friend always ready to do the disagreeable things for one," Mrs. Brown said.

"But I like to make buttonholes," protested Carrie.

"Nevertheless, we cannot always escape unpleasant things," Mrs. Brown continued remorselessly, " good - bys, for instance. We shall all miss you, Professor Bainbridge," and she extended her hand to him, " but these young ladies will feel your loss greatly." She spoke collectively, but she looked at Ethel.

"Yes," Ethel returned indifferently, but with heightened color, " we shall miss Professor Bainbridge; it is always a pity to end a pleasant acquaintance. I suppose you know that I am to stay with the Swifts until Christmas, and that two patients are coming here from the Sanitarium next week? So the house will be fuller than ever."

" And you are here to speed the parting and welcome the coming guest, Miss Ethel," Mrs. Brown said, by way of a gracious farewell, as she and Miss Harwood took their leave.

Carrie saw a pained expression on the professor's face, and hastened to observe with warmth, " We shall all miss you dreadfully, Mr. Bainbridge, and the new people won't in the least take your place."

He gave her a grateful look; in a moment he had conjured up a vision of the ideal woman who should have Carrie's transparent sincerity, unswerving loyalty, and unselfishness, joined to Ethel's beauty and fascination. But alas! in this imperfect world the man with keen insight into character never comes across those perfect combinations which his vivid imagination invents, and his less discerning brethren think that they have found; and there are moments when the compensation of being able to see the good points in a Mrs. Brown cannot make up to him for feeling the flaws in those he loves.

After their guests had departed, Ethel rose quickly and, seating herself at the piano, she played one piece after another at the professor's request. There was a minor strain in them all. Carrie grew more and more restless and sad as she listened, until she could bear it no longer; she did not know what troubled her, but she had suddenly become aware of the misery in the world. How could Ethel help loving him? And since she did not, why must she increase his pain by playing this heart-breaking music, and by looking so wonderfully lovely in her white gown, with the candlelight shining on her golden-brown hair, and the deepening color in her cheeks.

"Have I played all your favorites to you now?" Ethel asked after a time. "It is your last chance." She cast down her eyes, and added in a lower tone, "I hope we shall not lose sight of you forever."

"Forever!" exclaimed the professor impetuously, his resentment and doubts alike forgotten.

It was at this moment that Carrie left the room. She waited in the dark, upstairs, for a long time. At length Ethel came.

She moved softly, for she thought that Carrie was asleep.

"You can light the candle, Ethel; I have not gone to bed, I am over here on the sofa," Carrie said. Ethel crossed the room, and taking a seat by her friend's side, she felt for her hand. This unusual demonstration gave Carrie a sudden pang.

"Carrie, how do you like Mr. Bainbridge?" Ethel asked abruptly.

"Very much, but it would be more to the purpose if I were to ask you how *you* like him."

Ethel was silent a moment; then she said, with a thrill in her voice that Carrie never forgot, "How do I like him? Very well, — that is, — to-night — I am engaged to him."

There was a dull pain at Carrie's heart all the next day, which grew more intense as the hour for Mr. Bainbridge's departure approached. She was too busy all the morning to allow herself the luxury of thought. In the afternoon the house was overrun with people; there were visitors in the parlor and children everywhere else. She went into the garden, but retreated quickly, for Ethel and the professor were in the summer-house. Then she wended her way to the barn to tell Jerry to be sure to harness the horse in time for Mr. Bainbridge, who was to leave on the five o'clock train. Yielding to a sudden impulse she climbed up into the loft and settled herself comfortably in the hay as she used to do when she was a little girl. She wished she were a little girl now; life was hard for grown-up people.

Why was it she did not rejoice in Ethel's engagement? she asked herself. What did these strange feelings mean? Surely she had never fancied in her wildest dreams that Mr. Bainbridge might love herself. Her face grew hot at the thought. Then why was she not glad that he was to marry her friend? She was a selfish, jealous girl, for she would have liked to keep his friendship exclusively. For a moment she let herself imagine what it would be to have his love when she had found the crumbs of kindliness which had fallen to her share so pleasant; for a moment she felt how she might have loved him; then she dismissed such reflections as useless. He and Ethel were happy, and it was right that they should be so, for he loved her, and she was beautiful and good. "Much better than I am," thought poor Carrie. "I am not only plain and tiresome, but horrid too."

Through the open doors of the barn she could see Mrs. Brown and Miss Harwood walking down the village street and pausing to talk to her uncle, the doctor, who was just going into the sanitarium. It was what had happened a hundred times before, and it had seemed sufficiently interesting once; but now it was inexpressibly dreary to think of the days stretching on interminably with only such events in them for her.

"I wonder what I was put into the world for?" she thought. "And the worst of it is, I am not the only one; I could bear it better if I were. There must be thousands of commonplace people like me, who are not interesting enough to be fallen in love with, but who have hearts of their own just the same. Of course they can't get what they want, and all they can do is to *try* to be glad that some people can. After all it is true, what Mr. Bainbridge said the other night when I got so angry, — that I am of use in this family. I suppose some people are needed just to fill up gaps and make it easier for the others. That idea ought to content me, but somehow it doesn't. Well, any way, I am glad for them."

When she reached the house, the carriage that was to take Mr. Bainbridge to the depot was standing at the door, and he was about to help in Ethel, who was to drive him to the station. Carrie went up to them and extended both her hands impulsively.

"I have not had a chance to congratulate you together before," she said, "but I am so very, very glad."

They took her sympathy as a matter of course, and were too much absorbed in their happiness to notice the expression that for a moment glorified her plain face.

"Fortunate people!" Carrie thought as they drove away. "It can't be very hard for them to part, for they belong to each other."

She stood watching them until they were out of sight, and then she went into the house, to mend and put away the clean clothes.

A BISMARCK DINNER

The celebrated historian, Julius Franklin, was to deliver his lecture on Bismarck, in the Town Hall at Eastville, on the twenty-third of January, and he was to spend the night with the Frank Morses.

Mrs. Morse was a pretty little thing, who won from her serious neighbors when she came as a bride to Eastville, first, an amused tolerance, and later, a sincere affection; for despite the general opinion, a pretty woman, if she is also good-natured, makes her way more readily than a plain one with her own sex as well as with men. As Eastville was a New England town it is hardly necessary to add that it was populated chiefly with Mrs. Morse's sex. The women were for the most part studious and thoughtful, taking life seriously, as if they felt it incumbent upon them to cultivate their minds to the utmost, that the usual ill effects of the scarcity of the masculine element might be reduced to their minimum. The work done in the Ladies' Literary Guild was therefore of a thorough quality. Every winter the researches of this society were supplemented with a course of lectures given by literary lights from the outer world, but Julius Franklin's fame as surely eclipsed that of his predecessors as sunlight eclipses candlelight. It was therefore small wonder that the usually dauntless Edith Morse was frightened when she thought of the rapidly approaching twenty-third of January.

One morning she entered the library where her husband was comfortably ensconced in his leathern armchair before the open fire, with a pile of law books on a table near at hand.

"Frank," she began, "I am sorry to interrupt you, but you must help me, for Bismarck is more important than law."

"That is certainly his own opinion, my dear," Mr. Morse returned, putting down, not Blackstone, but one of Gaboriau's novels.

"I want you to tell me what to have for dinner on the twenty-third," Edith proceeded. "The dreadful day will be here in a week. What do you suppose a lecturer on Bismarck would like for dinner?"

"You might give him the Diet of Frankfort; he would be sure to feel at home then."

"Frank, it is cruel of you to joke in this way," she remonstrated; "this is a serious matter."

"Happily everything is a serious matter with you, Edith, my love. It is an immense comfort to me that I have married a woman who takes life thoughtfully. I must confess, however, that your pretty clothes and your beauty are a drawback; they create a false impression at the start, making one feel that you are only a butterfly."

"Frank," she continued, ignoring this remark, "don't you think that it will be best to have dinner at half-past four, as Mr. Franklin is coming on the half-past three train? If we had a six o'clock dinner he would be almost famished by that time; and as everybody dines at one o'clock here, it won't be any queerer to

A BISMARCK DINNER

have dinner at half-past four than at six. I wish I could think of something original to eat."

"Why not have it a Bismarck dinner? Pink teas are all the rage, but a Bismarck dinner in Bismarck-brown would be something new."

"The very thing!" Edith exclaimed, and she kissed her husband with rapturous effusion. "Who but you would have thought of such a lovely idea! After all, in spite of Miss Elliott, I do believe that men have more brain than women."

Frank Morse had thrown out his suggestion by way of the wildest joke; but if a man has married a woman who regards his lightest word with veneration he must take the consequences.

"A Bismarck dinner will be perfectly charming," said Edith. "I can have black bean soup for the first course — that is n't just the shade, but it is near enough to pass — and some kind of fried fish afterwards; then grouse and potato balls, — I shall have to omit the jelly and the salad too, — and then chocolate ice-cream, and after that, fruit. What fruit is there that is brown? Oh, yes, nuts, nuts and — I can't have raisins — well, nuts, all by themselves, and to wind up with — coffee. Who could help liking such a ménu? Then to make the table look pretty I will paint dinner-cards with appropriate designs."

"The Battle of Königgratz would be an easy illustration to begin with," her husband suggested.

"Frank, how can you propose such impossible things! How many people ought we to ask, do you think? I can't invite the whole guild, because there are twenty of them; and besides, I should like for once to have an even number of ladies and gentlemen."

"Then your dinner-party will limit itself."

"I think ten people will be enough," she said, as she flitted away to look through the Life of Bismarck for ideas for her dinner-cards.

Mrs. Morse was supposed to have read two lives of her hero, besides several magazine articles on the subject; but as she believed in judicious skipping, the chief events in Bismarck's life were somewhat vague in her mind. She wanted an allusion to each of these on the dinner-cards. She knew that the acquisition of Schleswig and Holstein was one of the important facts in his career, but how the annexation of that territory came about was not clear to her. Her impression was briefly this: Bismarck wanted the provinces, and somehow or other he obtained them; and it is possible that this condensed summary of the facts was not so unlike the knowledge of her superiors in quality as in quantity. She was also aware that there had been a war between Prussia and Austria, but she had not the smallest idea what it was about or which side was victorious, and neither could she tell the direct cause of the Franco-Prussian war, although she had an indistinct idea that either Spain or Italy was mixed up with it.

If Edith Morse's information concerning the principal events in her favorite's career was slight, on the other hand she had an intimate acquaintance with him on the personal side. She thought him a charming brother and a delightful husband, and she wished that Frank would take pattern by him and present his wife with an opal heart. It was also firmly impressed upon her mind that once when the Ex-Chancellor was a student, he taught punctuality to his shoemaker by sending a commissionnaire, at six o'clock in the morning of the day when his boots were promised him, to inquire if they were done, and when he found, according to his expectations, that this was not the case, that he sent messenger after messenger at intervals of half an hour, until the frantic shoemaker finished the boots in season to be worn to a party that evening. Unfortunately these facts did not lend themselves kindly to decorative purposes. An opal heart on a dinner-card might be subject to misinterpretation, and a pair of boots could not be made artistic. At last, in despair, Edith implored her husband to design the dinner-cards.

He promptly suggested, as a motto for the first course, " Bismarck is in the soup," but his wife frowned upon him, and, gathering her books of reference together, she placed them in a pile before him.

"You must not stir from this spot until you have found me suitable mottoes," she commanded.

"Here is a good motto for your course of nuts, which, it must be owned, seems rather slender without raisins," he said presently in triumph. "You will only have to quote Bismarck's memorable words, 'Far from sufficient.'"

At this juncture Miss Elliott was opportunely announced, and Edith went into the parlor to relate her trials to her. She was a clever, sarcastic woman, whose chief ambition was to know distinguished people, and who was consequently much gratified at receiving an invitation to dine with the illustrious Mr. Franklin.

"It will be a rare treat, my dear," she said. "And it was very sweet of you to think of including me."

Edith proceeded to confide her plans for the dinner-cards to her friend, who at once solved her difficulties by suggesting that she should paint the trefoil and the oak-leaves on the Bismarck coat-of-arms, in sepia, in the right-hand corner of each card, and tie a bow of Bismarck-brown ribbon in the left-hand corner.

"Dear Miss Elliott," cried Edith with enthusiasm, "you are an angel. You shall sit next to Mr. Franklin at dinner, and ask him questions on every subject."

She thought it safest to generalize.

"I have heard from my friends the Ainsworths that Mr. Franklin is a brilliant talker, and a mine of information," said her visitor. "I am impatient for next Friday to arrive."

Poor Mrs. Morse did not share this impatience, but trembled more and more as the dreaded day approached.

It came at last, bringing the distinguished stranger with it.

Mr. Franklin was an angular little man of about fifty-five, with grizzled hair and small gray eyes which looked irritably at the world through a pair of gold-bowed spectacles.

As Mrs. Morse showed him to his room she remarked that dinner would be ready in half an hour.

The guests arrived with commendable

A BISMARCK DINNER

promptness and began at once to adapt their conversation to the great occasion.

"I understand that you have made a thorough study of Bismarck, Mrs. Morse," said Mr. Parke, a young man who was deeply interested in German history.

Edith glanced at the clock. It was time to send the maid to let Mr. Franklin know that dinner was ready.

"Bismarck seems to me a remarkably charming person," she said, with a pretty little air of authority. "It was a surprise to me to find that he was so lovable in his family."

"I was not thinking of him as an individual, but as a factor in history," Mr. Parke rejoined. "It would be interesting to look ahead fifty years to see whether Germany's progress was retarded or advanced by his measures. What is your opinion of his course with regard to the May Laws?"

Edith groped vainly in her memory for some facts concerning these laws. "I think his connection with the Franco-Prussian war was more noteworthy," she said, with one of her charming smiles.

"Of course. Have you been reading Busch and Lowe?"

"Yes."

"Then you must remember the account of the battle of Sedan, and the interview between Napoleon and Bismarck afterwards. Is it not exceedingly vivid?"

"Very vivid," she said fervently, although all that she could remember about it was that the Emperor wore white kid gloves and was smoking a cigarette. "Excuse me for a moment," she added hastily, as she went to tell Agatha to summon Mr. Franklin.

Upon her return to the parlor she seated herself at the other side of the room from the terrifying Mr. Parke, but he crossed over and continued the interrupted conversation. Fortunately for those people whose aim it is to go through life without exposing their ignorance there is an equally large class of persons whose chief desire is to show their knowledge.

Mr. Parke was a member of this fraternity, and his companion's interest was sufficient to encourage him to expound

A BISMARCK DINNER

his views on State Socialism at great length.

"Bismarck is a wonderful man," she said sapiently, in a pause which demanded some remark from her.

"It is a pity that he should have grown so garrulous in his old age," Mr. Parke observed.

Edith knew nothing about the latter part of Bismarck's career, for the "lives" had stopped short of this period, but, given the smallest cue, this young woman could improvise her part.

"Don't you think that elderly people almost always become garrulous?" she asked, with a confiding smile.

"Yes, it is the tendency of old age. What do *you* think of Bismarck's attitude toward State Socialism? I should like to know what an intelligent woman, unbiased by party prejudice and untrammeled by previous views, would make of it."

"I fear I am not unbiased," Edith said hurriedly, being also afraid that she was not an intelligent woman. It was quarter of five. What had become of

Agatha? Here she was at the parlor door now.

"You must have some opinion of Bismarck's high-handed course," Mr. Parke urged.

"It was, as you say, high handed, very high handed," she said, as she abruptly left the room.

"Please, ma'am," began Agatha, "Mr. Franklin is a little deaf, and I could n't make him understand at first, but as soon as he see what I was driving at he said he did n't want any dinner."

Mrs. Morse looked aghast. "What did you say then?" she asked faintly.

"'There's ladies and gentlemen to meet you,' says I, 'and they'll be terrible disappointed.' 'I can't help that,' says he, 'I want to read over my lecture.'"

Mrs. Morse returned to the parlor in a subdued frame of mind, and sent her husband to cope with the recreant historian. He returned, after a brief absence, unattended. She met him in the entry.

"Frank," she said reproachfully, "I

A BISMARCK DINNER

told you to be sure to bring Mr. Franklin."

"I know it, my dear, but there is a limit to human strength, and although he is small he must weigh at least a hundred and thirty-five pounds."

"This is no time for joking," she expostulated in tragic tones. "Won't he come down?"

"Not for me. You had better try your powers of persuasion."

They ascended the stairs together, and Edith knocked boldly on the historian's door.

"Who is there?" he asked gruffly.

"Mrs. Morse. Mr. Franklin," she added in her blandest tones, as he opened the door, "I know how kind you are and that you are always ready to do a good turn for people. Please put yourself in my place. I had dinner at this strange hour on purpose for you because I thought you would be hungry, and I have asked several friends to meet you. They have heard how delightful you are and they will never forgive me if they don't see you. Fancy dining at half-past four—

when we all dine at one generally — and without you. It is worse than the play of Hamlet with the ghost left out. What *are* you laughing at, Frank? Besides, I have arranged a little surprise for you; it is a Bismarck dinner."

"The only article of the kind, going — going," her husband murmured sotto voce.

"Madam," Mr. Franklin returned, "I am sorry to disappoint you, but I had a hearty lunch on the train at my usual dinner-hour. I have to be very careful in my diet, and therefore I can't eat anything now; but if you will give me a glass of milk and some toast, crisp brown toast, and a couple of baked apples at half-past six o'clock, I shall be greatly obliged to you."

"But, Mr. Franklin, even if you don't feel like eating anything, won't you sit at the table and talk to us while we are at dinner?"

"My dear madam, it is impossible, for I must read over my lecture."

"Miss Elliott is here," said Edith, playing her last card; "she is a friend of your friends the Ainsworths. Won't you come down just for a few minutes?" she begged.

"My dear madam, my nerves are in a sensitive condition, and it is imperative for me to have utter quiet until it is time for my lecture."

There was nothing more to be said, and Mrs. Morse took her place at the head of the dinner-table in an unusually chastened frame of mind, opposite her husband, who was ostentatiously merry, while the seven guests sipped their black bean soup, and tried to look as if they dined at half-past four every day.

After the tedious meal was over Edith had to give the historian his meagre repast. When she rejoined her guests in the parlor she was besieged with a flow of questions.

"What did he say? Was he very interesting? Do tell us the whole conversation?" her friends demanded eagerly.

Edith looked up demurely. "I will tell you all about it," she said gravely.

She waited until the faces of her auditors had assumed the requisite amount of rapt attention, and then she began her narrative. "He said first, 'These apples are very good, Mrs. Morse, only I prefer them cold.'"

"Never mind these irrelevant details," said Miss Elliott impatiently. "Go on to the interesting part."

"But there was n't any interesting part; it was all about what he could eat, and what he could n't eat, and what he would like to eat to-morrow."

"What did he say about Bismarck?" asked Mr. Parke.

"Not one word. It was heartless of him to stay in his room and spoil my dinner," poor Edith added plaintively.

"My dear, what better could he have done?" her husband inquired. "By reading over his lecture he was more in harmony with the occasion than he could have been in any other way."

"Why?"

"Because he was in a Bismarck-brown-study."

A HAMERTON TYPE-WRITER.

Richard Copley Armstrong, the rising young novelist, was sitting in his study in an attitude of profound thought. So absorbed was he, as he bent over his type-writer, that he did not hear the announcement of his maid-of-all-work that dinner was ready. This appellation, by the way, is scarcely the right one to apply to the buxom matron of fifty who stood in the doorway with her arms akimbo and shouted, "Dinner, dinner, Mr. Richard!"

The young man raised his head at last, and said thoughtfully, "U, I, O, P,— that stands for 'You I owe; patience.'"

"He's gone clean daft over that little machine of his'n," said the unsympathetic Mrs. Bassett. "Patience! that is certainly just what *is* needed in this house; but as for owing me, you don't; you paid me every stiver of my wages last Saturday night."

A HAMERTON TYPE-WRITER

Mr. Armstrong bent his head over the type-writer again, and murmured, " D, F, G, H ; or, ' darned fool, go home.' Oh, I had forgotten that you were here, Mrs. Bassett," he said good-naturedly. He had not been addressing her, — he was merely trying to learn the alphabet of his type-writer, by associating words with the letters.

That evening he struggled for a long time over a note to his friend, John Lawson. It was written on the type-writer, and ran as follows : —

Dear Hack,
i am in despaor/my eyes have guvem out utterly/ the oxxulist says i must not writ one word. i infested in this type-writer at his suggestion bevause i am in the niddle of my novel 2 AN EXperiment in CHArity ? " and the 2Metroopolis Maxagine 2is awaiting the next chapter. i am not allowed even too look at what i writ or at the type)writer ketters thenselves, but am lerning to use the mavine as the blinddo. so if there are one or two mistakes in this epistel forgibe them. MRs. BAssett is too illiter ate to help me. i have learned the letters from a man from the oggice of the 2Ham-

erton type)write2 so alli need is a little practise ? vut it has taken me || hours to accomplish this brief note. for the love of heavem come and stay with me and be my ammennuensus until iget the nest number of my novek finixhed/

your devoted fiend ,
richard COpley armstrong/
december $th, 1 ' ' (/

He received the following answer by return of mail : —

Dear richard : —

I adopt the small " r " since you so evidently prefer it. I am very, very sorry, my poor, devoted " fiend," but your dear old " literary ? " hack is too deep in his own work to be able to spare any time for you. I wish he could. I will suggest that you get a professional type-writer to come to you every day until your novel is finished. Don't delude yourself, my dear boy, into thinking that you will be able to do work fit for the press, on your type-writer, alone and unassisted.

Regretfully yours,

JACK.

P. S. The date of your letter is charmingly mysterious, and suggests that you have been sojourning in eternity rather than time.

A HAMERTON TYPE-WRITER

As the outgrowth of the proposition made by John Lawson, a young lady came every morning at ten o'clock to the study of Richard Armstrong, and worked there patiently for three hours. I say patiently advisedly; for although Richard was generally a charming companion and was thought fascinating by all women, fascination is not a quality that tells in a man when he has a rooted dislike to dictation and a nervous temperament.

After a week of progress in company with the amanuensis, Richard received a letter from his friend containing these inquiries:—

Why do you never mention the type-writer? Is she satisfactory?

In answer, the exasperated Richard wrote the following note:—

Dear Jack :)
Will you be so hood as to remember in future that i am not allowed to use my eyes at all, and so can8t read my motes. Your letters have to be fead to me either by the type-write herself, or by my AUNT Hammah whose house i am manning at present. This excel-

lent lady read your last epidle and was hoffifoed. AS she is going away for two months miss grey will read the others. miss GRey is not pretty. She is nothing but a machine, a verry usefull skilful? and caluable Hamerton type-write, but no more. i think o of her as a part of the mavhine she works. It is a signifidant fact that both have the same appellattion? both are type-writes.

Yours in great haste,
dick/

p/s/ Have i not improved greatly in my type-writing?
DEcemberi&th.

It was true that Miss Grey was not pretty, but she had a charming face and simple, unobtrusive manners. She came day after day and took her place quietly in Richard's study, never talking unless she were addressed, but when she was consulted always suggesting some way of disentangling the knotty problem under discussion. Her voice was low and agreeable, and she was altogether a pleasant feature in Richard's solitary life. After a time he grew to look forward to her daily appearance, and to take a certain interest in her personality. He could not help himself; every woman interested him more or less, from his great-aunt down to the little girl who brought him his weekly washing. Miss Grey was far from being the contemporary of his aunt; she could not be more than twenty-five or six.

At the end of a fortnight Miss Grey and Mr. Armstrong had accomplished the number of his novel for which the "Metropolis Magazine" had been waiting so impatiently.

"I suppose you will not want me any longer," she said, as she put on her jacket and gloves preparatory to taking her departure.

"Indeed I shall; I am not going to get myself into such another tight box with my next number. I shall want you straight on until the end of the chapter — the novel, I mean."

"Monday is Christmas," she reminded him, "so you probably will not care to have me come again for some days. I wish you a very merry Christmas," she added, as she extended her hand to him.

"I am not going home," he rejoined, keeping her hand absently in his for a moment, and then dropping it with a sigh; "and I shall not have a merry Christmas, but on the contrary a signally dismal one. Come on Christmas and help me to get through with the day," he went on rapidly. He could see that her eyes were beautiful as well as kind, as she raised them to his with a questioning glance.

"I am sorry that you cannot go home," she said.

"I do not wish to go home," he returned quickly; "I don't want to be reminded of last Christmas."

Had Miss Grey expressed a keen interest in his revelations, it is probable that the young man would have stopped making them; but she said nothing more, and yet he knew that she was sorry for him, and because of this fact, and for the reason that he had received no sympathy for a long time, he felt impelled to proceed.

"Last Christmas I was engaged," he said, "but the girl whom I was to marry has married another man."

Afterward he thought what a fool he

had been to tell this fact in his history to his amanuensis; and why, at least, could he not have accomplished the feat gracefully, instead of blurting it out in that school-boy fashion? He attacked his typewriter with virulence. D, F, stood emphatically for what he was himself, and it was with peculiar satisfaction that he said over and over again, "Darned fool, *darned fool*, go home."

His studies were interrupted at this point by Mrs. Bassett, who had thrust her bulky person into the range of his vision.

"Yes, sir," she said; "you've called me a 'darned fool' once too often; I'm taking of your advice, sir; I'm 'going home.'"

"Mrs. Bassett!" he cried, aghast, "I can't get along without you. I was not speaking to you; I was merely addressing the type-writer."

"It's all the same thing, sir. There is one 'fool' in this house, that's sure. If it's me, I'd better leave; but if it's you, — why, I never calculated to get along with folly. Since that machine come, you've ben clean crazy. Take your choice. Keep your Hamerton type-writer, or keep me. Give it up, or give me up. I won't live in the same house with the uncanny thing any longer."

He took his choice, and as a consequence Mrs. Bassett departed, and the Hamerton type-writer remained.

On Christmas morning Richard Armstrong was almost too ill to get up. He managed, however, to stagger downstairs to his study. He laid his wretched feelings to the poorly cooked food which had followed upon Mrs. Bassett's departure. When Miss Grey came in the afternoon, she found him flushed and feverish, and in great pain.

"You must not try to work," she said, "and you must let me go for a doctor. I am afraid you have the grippe."

Richard, however, insisted upon dictating, as he said his brain had never been so full of ideas. He grew more and more excited as they worked, until Frances Grey became seriously alarmed. Finally, she heard a dull thud, and upon looking in his direction she saw that he had fallen to the floor in a dead faint. She was now thoroughly frightened. She was a sufficiently good nurse to succeed in restoring her patient to partial consciousness, but almost as soon as he came out of his faint turn he grew delirious.

Mr. Armstrong and Miss Grey were alone in the house, and therefore she could not leave him to go for a doctor. What should she do? How could she obtain aid? She glanced at the tall, old-fashioned clock, whose hands were pointing to five minutes of four. She had not realized that they had worked so long, but twilight was in fact fast approaching, and she ought to be starting for home.

She ran to the front window, and shouted "Help! help!" at the top of her voice. No response came, for Richard Armstrong lived in a house with as much land around it as if it were not situated in one of the nearest suburbs of a great city. She rang a bell which she found in the dining-room, but even its insistent peals produced no effect. After this she went back into the study to look at her patient, who was moaning and tossing restlessly on the sofa. At last she ran down the long avenue at full speed, crying, "Help, help!"

A little boy was sauntering past on the other side of the street. He eyed her with interest.

"Is it a fire or a murder, Missis?" he asked.

"A gentleman is very ill," she said. "I will give you this half-dollar if you will go for the nearest doctor, and tell him to come here immediately, to this house,— you understand?—to see Mr. Richard Armstrong."

Half an hour passed, then another half-hour, and still another; yet neither boy nor doctor appeared. The tall old mahogany clock in the corner was striking six in its silvery voice. A clock seems so alive and companionable, that it is a disappointment to find it strikes in the same bland unvarying way when we ourselves are racked with anxiety. Frances Grey was tempted to stop the timepiece, that its measured, dignified ticking and its imperturbable striking might cease.

It was now as dark as if it were midnight. Miss Grey realized that there was little chance of her being rescued by her friends; for her landlady would think that she had gone directly to the house of Mrs. Grant, where she had promised to assist at some Christmas festivities. Laura Grant, on the other hand, would imagine that she was belated in some way, and would not feel anxious about her. Self-reliance was not an inborn quality with Frances, but an acquired one; and she felt very lonely and helpless as she sat in Mr. Armstrong's study, watching his irregular breathing, and wondering whether the simple remedies at her command had been the right ones.

Half-past six, and still no doctor! She would make one more effort to secure a messenger. She was about putting on her fur cape when she heard a stifled voice from the sofa.

"Don't go," Richard begged. "Q, W, E, R, T, Y, — Queen, worthy, that's how I remember the letters, — worthy Queen, my Queen, don't go. U, I, O, P, patience. A, S, darned fool, go, — no, that is not so good as the other; what is the other?" He pressed his hand wearily to his head. "I have it now," he said at last: "Dear Frances Grey, heavenly jabberer, or was it jackknife? Don't go, heavenly jabberer."

Frances sank into an armchair and laughed hysterically.

"I am coming back," she said gently, when she had recovered her voice.

Richard, however, seized her hand, and would not let her go. Throughout all his delirious wanderings it seemed to comfort him to feel her presence.

The moments were like hours to Frances, and the hours like days. It was now eight o'clock, and she began to wonder if she would have to spend a long night alone with her charge. Could the boy have proved faithless? He had an honest face.

At length, just before nine o'clock, she heard the welcome sound of wheels on the gravel outside, and presently the doctor entered the room. He had been too busy with cases of grippe to come any earlier in the day. He was a bluff and burly old gentleman, with a kind face, but a rough manner. He examined the patient carefully and listened to a description of his symptoms given by Miss Grey.

"It is a case of grippe," he said; "a very extreme case, aggravated by some mental trouble. What has he on his mind?"

"The Hamerton type-writer," the patient moaned; "the best in the market, the most easily mastered by those who cannot see. Only one set of letters, but you must be careful to press the stop for the capitals Z, X, C, V, 'Zealous Xerxes collects violins;' that's how I remember them; but the question-marks and the periods are the hardest."

The doctor left the usual prescriptions for grippe, and promised to call again on the following morning.

"I think your brother is not going to be very ill," he said kindly.

"He is no relation of mine," said Miss Grey, "and not even a friend. I am merely his amanuensis, and I am alone in the house with him. You *must* send a nurse."

"It is impossible," the doctor rejoined. "All the nurses are engaged. I have not been able to get hold of one all day."

Frances implored him to at least find some woman to keep her company, that she might not have to bear the strain of a solitary, anxious night. "We ought to telegraph to his mother," she suggested.

"Yes," Dr. Marston agreed, "and I will send the telegram if you will write it out for me."

Frances sank helplessly into a chair. "I do not know in what part of the world she lives," she explained. "We will ask him; perhaps he may tell us, in a moment of intelligence."

The doctor approached Richard, and said distinctly, "Where does your mother live?"

The young man looked at him blandly, and murmured, with a beaming smile, his favorite refrain, "Darned fool, go home."

"Look here," said the doctor, "I won't be insulted."

"He is wandering in his mind, poor fellow!" Frances said. "I will ask him."

She came close to him, and said gently, "Mr. Armstrong, it is I, Miss Grey, the type-writer."

"Best machine in the market," he muttered.

"Yes, the Hamerton is the best," she said soothingly; "but we are talking of your mother, Mrs. Armstrong. Where does she live?"

"Be sure to press your interrogations, or you will get a figure 2," he observed in a confiding tone; "a figure 2 looks badly in the manuscript."

"It is of no use," Frances said, with a sigh; "we must find out his mother's address in some other way."

"J, K, L stands for John Kingsley Lawson," Richard murmured.

"That is true. We can send the message through his friend, Mr. Lawson," she suggested, "and ask him to forward the news to Mrs. Armstrong."

That was the longest night that Frances ever spent. The doctor sent one of his own servants to stay with her, but the woman was too frightened and inexperienced to be of any assistance. Mr. Armstrong was delirious the greater part of the night, but at length he fell into a troubled sleep, from which he would awake every few moments, to mutter crazy ejaculations, or to seize Miss Grey's hand and beg her not to leave him. "Please stay, dear fool, until the end of the chapter," he said over and over again.

"Of course I will stay," Frances answered kindly, "as long as you want me; to the very last of the book, and it is going to be a great novel."

Toward morning he awoke again, and his mind seemed clearer. "Have I been very ill?" he asked. "My head is a trifle confused. I hope I was quite polite."

"You were — most considerate," Frances replied in reassuring tones. It was a small matter to have been addressed in uncivil language by a man whose heart was in the right place, if his head were in the wrong one.

He sighed. "I am glad; I am very glad. I thought I might possibly have called you a 'darn ——' but it's all right since I did n't."

A sharp spasm of pain seized him. He

looked up with a wan smile. "You promised to stay with me to the end of the chapter," he said faintly. "Perhaps it is nearer being finished than we thought; perhaps it is time to write THE END now."

"Oh, no," said Frances, bending over him with a tearful face; "you will be better, and your novel will be finished, and your mother is coming to-morrow."

He did get better. There were many weary days first, during which his mother and the doctor and Miss Grey had anxious hearts, although they tried to keep cheerful faces; but at last he grew well enough to take his place again in the study, and to begin to work on his novel.

Mrs. Armstrong was a fragile little woman, with too much sentiment for the comfort of her friends, and with the certainty that her son was the only really great American novelist. She was so fond of him that she was jealous of any other influence, and was morally certain that she could be his amanuensis quite as satisfactorily as his new friend. She had overpowered Frances by her gratitude and affection so long as Richard's life hung in the balance; but when he was well on the way to recovery, she dismissed her in a somewhat cavalier fashion.

Richard had inherited his nervous temperament from his mother, and under the joint management of the mother and son the book remained at a standstill, and Mrs. Armstrong was at last forced reluctantly to admit that it might be best to send for the "type-writer," as otherwise the public would have to wait indefinitely for the completion of "the most glorious American novel." Miss Grey therefore was at last summoned, and she came at once, with no apparent feeling of ill-will, and took her place as quietly in the corner of the study as if she had never left it. She found Richard sitting in the large easy-chair, "himself again," although a little pale and thin.

"How good it is to get you back again!" he said, with one of his bright smiles. "I have missed you more than you would believe possible."

He watched her every motion with the same deep satisfaction with which a little boy bends his gaze on his good mamma who has chanced to be absent for a time. What attractive ways she had, and what a charming face! She was a woman whom any man might be proud to call his mother, or his sister; for she would be ideal in either relation. Only a very exceptional man would fall in love with her, Richard thought; for his sex in general is captivated by external charm, or a lively, fascinating manner. To love this woman, one must be on the farther side of an experience which had shown one the deceitfulness of mere personal charm. Richard felt himself to be the one uncommon man who appreciated her.

He began to dictate. They had reached a somewhat dry part of the story, or at least a portion which depended for its interest on delicacy of touch rather than startling incident. The hero, Miles Grecourt, had come to a critical point in his experiment in charity. He had set up a small ragamuffin in the trade of bootblacking, notwithstanding the urchin's frequently expressed preference for another way of life, and he was now being rewarded by ingratitude.

"'You're an old humbug,' said the quasi-bootblack," Richard dictated, "'goin' around the world thinkin' to do folkses such a pile of good by makin' 'em happy in your way rather than their own. Now, as I told you, I've always had the dream of bein' a newspaper boy, but you insisted upon my bein' a bootblack'"— Richard paused to give Miss Grey time to finish this sentence. "It is of no use," he went on; "I love you in spite of everything. I may say to myself that it is only that I am dependent on you, but I cheat myself with words; I love you, I love you!"

Miss Grey's fingers flew rapidly over the keys, but she said, "Do you think that last sentence in character?"

"In character!" Richard repeated savagely; "and pray why is it not in character?"

"Because I do not see why the bootblack changed his mind so suddenly."

"The bootblack! Hang the bootblack! I am talking of myself and of you."

"And I am waiting for you to dictate

the next paragraph," Frances said in icy tones. Her hands were on the keyboard of the type-writer. Richard seized the one that was nearest him.

"Look here, Miss Grey, will you listen quietly to what I have to say, and let that confounded machine alone?"

"Yes, Mr. Armstrong, if you, on your side, will remember that I am 'only a type-writer.'"

His very words, — but how could she have heard them? He must have said them in his delirium.

"Miss Grey," he went on, with a little break in his voice, "whatever I may have said when I was not myself, the fact remains that I love you; I have had dreary days without you; I cannot tell" —

"No, you cannot, you must not tell me any more. Believe me, I never dreamed of this. I have liked you as a brother from the very first, because, — I could not tell you then, for it was a secret, — and afterwards Jack sent me a part of your letter, and as you thought of me as 'only a type-writer,' it seemed simpler to go on as we had begun. Do you understand **now**? **It was** through Mr. Lawson that I **came to you.**"

"So you are a **friend of Jack's**. He might have had the grace **to tell** me so in the beginning; but my dearest" —

"You do not understand. **I am** engaged to Jack Lawson."

One ray of hope was **still left to** Richard.

"You are engaged to be his amanuensis, — his type-writer?" he inquired.

"I am engaged to be married to him; I have promised to stay with him 'to the **end** of the chapter.'"

A FAITHFUL FAILURE

The journey from New York to Hamilton, New Hampshire, can be made in seven hours, a period of time which may or may not be long to the passengers, according to circumstances. To Maurice Wentworth, a man of nearly forty, who was traveling over the road for the first time in many years, the journey seemed interminable, for he occupied himself in reviewing the events that had taken place since he and his brother were boys in Hamilton, and this exercise of mind was not conducive to cheerful thoughts. How often, as a lad, he had watched the train steam away from the Hamilton station into an unknown world, with the determination strong within him to win a distinguished place in that world! And now it was bringing him back as poor and unknown as he had been when it had taken him away! "I am nothing but 'a faithful failure,'" he said to himself bitterly, borrowing a phrase from Stevenson.

His brother, on the other hand, was unusually prosperous, and Maurice asked himself if Robert's apparent selfishness had not been justified by results. If he had pushed his fortunes with little regard to the rights of others, he was now in a position to hold out a helping hand to the less favored, for he was rich, influential, and happily married; while he, the elder brother, was alone in the world, and coming, at Robert's invitation, to spend the summer with him in the old homestead, while waiting for some opening by which he could earn his living.

"East Hamilton!" called the conductor, breaking in upon his reflections.

Hamilton was the next station, and Wentworth looked out of the open window at the familiar scenery, and saw that here, at least, nothing had changed while the fortunes of men were being made or marred. As he glanced at the half-wooded hills that encircled the horizon, and at the river rushing tumultuously over its rocky channel, now hidden in

A FAITHFUL FAILURE

the woods, only to flash into life again when there was a gap in the forest, it seemed but yesterday since he had gone over this same road, an eager, hopeful boy.

Meanwhile, Robert Wentworth and his wife, who were driving down to the station to meet their relative, reviewed his career after their own fashion.

"Maurice is such a good fellow that it is a pity he hasn't a little more push," said Mrs. Wentworth.

"A little more?" her husband returned. "I should be devoutly grateful if he had any."

"Robert, I can't bear to have you say such things about your brother, for he is so nice to the children."

"Yes, taking care of children is his forte. If he were a woman, he could earn his living as a nursery-maid."

"How unkind of you! He is a very bright man, and would have made a brilliant lawyer, I have no doubt, if it hadn't been for the trouble with his eyes."

"Charlotte, a man who is bound to

succeed will succeed, even if the Lord and the devil are both against him, and a man who is bound to fail will fail. I believe in predestination to that extent. The trouble with Maurice's eyes need n't have made his ranch life a failure. Do you suppose I should make a failure of ranch life if I were obliged to try it?"

"No dear," his wife said soothingly. "I don't think you could fail at anything."

They reached the Hamilton station as she spoke, and the next moment the brother who owned that he had failed was in the presence of the brother who owned that he had succeeded.

Robert saw a tall man come forward to meet him, with an air of gentlemanly shabbiness, and a face full of careworn lines, which, together with his gray hair, made him look ten years older than his actual age. It irritated him to find that Maurice showed so plainly the marks of having passed a cheerless and unprosperous life, and his vexation was increased by the fact that he bore a strong family likeness to himself. Maurice, on the other hand, was struck by the fact that his brother had scarcely changed in the last ten years. He was as handsome as ever, and showed unmistakably that the world had lavished its best gifts upon him. Maurice saw, too, a vivacious little woman, with sparkling black eyes, sparkling diamond earrings, a wealth of red roses on her leghorn hat, a rainbow of colors in her gown, and a cascade of fluttering ribbons.

"I am so glad to see you, Maurice," she said with a cordiality that was very grateful to the lonely man. "The children have talked of nothing but your coming for days. They enjoyed your visit in New York so much. It was a pity that Robert lost it! And to think that you boys have n't seen each other for ten years!"

Their way led through the town of Hamilton, with its long, elm-lined main street and its straggling group of shops and wooden churches, and then uphill for two miles until they reached the Wentworth farm.

Here Maurice and his brother had lived

when they were boys, and here Robert spent his summers, having remodeled the old homestead, and turned it into a comfortable modern dwelling. As they approached the red house under the elm-trees, a bevy of small girls, headed by a little boy, ran down the road and presently surrounded the carriage.

"Uncle Maurice! How perfectly splendid that you have come!" exclaimed Beatrice, the eldest of the children.

"Guess what we have got in a barrel, uncle Maurice!" said Eleanor. "There are three of them, and their eyes have n't opened yet."

"They must be chickens," he observed solemnly.

"Chickens in a barrel! How funny you are, uncle Maurice!"

By this time their uncle had descended from the wagon and was going along the gravel path toward the porch, his left hand seized by Eleanor, and his valise borne away in a determined manner by Beatrice and Bobby, while three little girls struggled to get possession of his disengaged hand.

"Don't quarrel so; leave your uncle in peace," their father said sternly.

The children, however, who had inherited their parent's determination, paid no heed to this remark, but dragged their guest into the house and out on the piazza. Here they deposited him in a cane-seated rocking-chair with broad arms; and the next moment he was buried beneath an avalanche of white gowns and streaming yellow hair. Marion, Carlotta, and Eleanor, the three younger children, contrived to climb into his lap, while Beatrice and Bobby perched on the arms of his chair, and the demure little Hester was forced to content herself with a chair drawn as close to her uncle as possible.

"Where is aunt Ellen? Go and find her, Hester," Beatrice commanded.

Hester, the only obedient child in this domineering and strong-willed family, slipped down from her chair and went in search of her aunt.

"It is so funny that you and aunt Ellen are n't any relation, when you are our uncle Maurice, and she is our aunt Ellen," mused Carlotta.

"Goosie, uncle Maurice can't be brother to papa and mamma both!" explained the superior Beatrice. "Aunt Ellen is awfully nice. Did you ever see her, uncle Maurice?"

"Not since she was about your size, Beatrice."

"She is grown up now."

"Not so awfully grown up," added Bobby. "Not so grown up as mamma."

"I am sorry she is grown up," Maurice owned, with a sigh. He could always count upon the affection of children, but he was not so sure of the approval of their elders.

"She is taller than mamma," Marion stated, "but I don't think she is so grown up in her mind, for she likes to make mud-pies."

He heard a pleasant, gentle laugh as his niece made this remark, and upon looking up he saw Ellen standing before him. He had a vivid impression of a personality that was altogether charming. He was sensitive to atmosphere, and he felt at once that this girl was uncritical, even shy and humble.

"I believe I don't mind so very much to find that you are grown up, Ellen," he said, as he shook hands with her.

In the days that followed, Maurice sometimes wished again that Ellen were a child, as in that case he could have had more chances to see her; for his time was spent chiefly with his nieces and nephew. In the minds of their parents the world was divided into two classes, — those persons who were fond of children and those who were not. They did not recognize any subtler distinctions, and realize that there are people who are fond of children for six hours, but not for sixteen, out of the twenty-four.

Maurice was sorry to find that Ellen had grown more reserved with her added years. He was especially struck with her shyness one evening when the Allens, a rich family in the neighborhood, were bidden to tea. The guests were taken out on the piazza until supper should be ready, for the day had been sultry. Mrs. Allen, fat, pompous, and dull, plied a palm-leaf fan, and listened to Mrs. Wentworth's vivacious chatter; her husband, fatter, more pompous, and duller, talked of farming with Robert; while their son, a slender blasé youth of twenty, adjusted his eyeglasses and patronized Ellen and the sunset. The poor girl devoutly hoped that she would be placed next to Maurice Wentworth at the tea-table, for he was the only one of the men with whom she felt she had anything in common. No such happy fate was hers, however. She was seated, as befitted her youth, next to Frank Allen, while her position as sister in the household gave her his father for her other neighbor. The old gentleman ignored her, and concentrated his attention upon his entertaining hostess. The younger man, pleased at first by her charming face, vouchsafed a few remarks, but soon made up his mind that she was as dull as her narrow life, in spite of her beautiful eyes. He presently relapsed into silence, which was broken only when Ellen, catching a disapproving glance from her brother-in-law, gathered courage to ask her neighbor some trivial question, which he answered by a monosyllable.

When the long-drawn agony was at last

over, and the guests had adjourned to the parlor, Robert captured Ellen as she was leaving the dining-room.

"Why did n't you talk to young Allen, instead of holding your tongue like a silly schoolgirl?" he demanded.

"I tried to talk to Mr. Allen," she answered humbly, "but he did not care for what I had to say," and she cast a hurried glance after Maurice, and wondered, in her self-abasement, if he had heard his brother's question.

"How can you expect any man to be interested in what you have to say when you are so doubtful about it yourself?" Robert inquired. "Dash in, Ellen. Say whatever comes into your head, as Charlotte does. That's the way to do it. Say it as if it were important, and every one will think it is important; but — above all — never look bored. Draw out the bores, Ellen, — that's the way to get on. You are pretty enough to succeed, if you will only take the trouble. I shall expect to hear you talking all the evening, whether you have anything to say or not."

A FAITHFUL FAILURE

When Robert left her, Ellen took refuge on the piazza to dry her eyes under shelter of the friendly darkness. She sat dejectedly in a corner, her depression extending itself even to the lines of her limp pink mull gown. Presently she heard a step, and before she could escape she saw Maurice at her elbow.

"Suppose we take a turn out here before we go into the parlor," he suggested. "We shall never be missed."

Ellen hastily tucked her handkerchief into her belt, and tried to steady her voice as she said, "It does n't matter about me, but you will be missed. You ought to go in."

"I missed!" He gave a short laugh. "Ellen," he asked, as they began to walk up and down the piazza, "what has my brother been saying to you? You look as forlorn as a rose that has been trodden underfoot."

"He wants me to be more like Charlotte. I wish I could be."

"It must be a comfort to be an average, conventional person," he assented, "ready at a moment's notice to adjust one's self

A FAITHFUL FAILURE

to fashion and circumstance. That is what it means to be successful."

"I should like to be successful," she admitted, "but I never can be, because I cannot talk. I am a great disappointment to Robert. He likes lively, bright people. I wish I could please him, for he has been so good to me. You know my home has been with him ever since aunt Martha went to live with aunt Ellen, when her husband died?"

"You were with your aunt Ellen the last time I saw you. What a quaint little girl you were! You could talk fast enough then."

"We really ought to go in," said the conscientious Ellen. "Robert will be displeased if we stay away."

"If you say so, we will; but we must sit together, Ellen, and then we need not talk unless we have something to say."

"Robert won't like it if I don't talk."

"Very well; then I will say to you at intervals, 'It is a pleasant evening,'— a great deal pleasanter out here, by the way, than in the house. Look at the mist on the mountains, and at that little crescent moon so clear-cut against the sky. It is a shame to go into the hot parlor when you and I could have such a nice time out here by ourselves. Society seems to be a device for making people uncomfortable."

"But we owe something to society, and we must go in," Ellen said firmly.

"We will go in, and whenever Robert's eye is upon us I will reiterate that it is a pleasant evening. He will be satisfied if he sees us talking, and you will merely have to say, 'Yes, it is a pleasant evening. I always did like hot drawing-rooms in summer weather.'"

Before the evening was over Ellen and Maurice had confided a number of things to each other, and they were soon laughing merrily; for whenever Robert looked that way, Maurice, true to his promise, no matter what subject they chanced to be discussing, broke off abruptly, and said with an excess of gravity to Ellen, "It is a pleasant evening."

That evening was the precursor of many that were equally delightful. The weeks slipped away, and Maurice ceased to think of his unhappy past and his precarious future, but gave himself up to the joys of a satisfying present. He had never known before the pleasure of easy and familiar intercourse with a young girl. It did not occur to him that he, middle-aged and penniless, might fall in love with Ellen; still less that she, beautiful and young, might grow to care for him; but he felt an unreasonable envy when he saw the comforts with which his brother had surrounded himself, and material things assumed the exaggerated value in his eyes which they often have for those of few possessions, who, because of their poverty, are erroneously supposed to despise comforts and luxuries. Had he been successful, he reasoned, he too might have had a happy home; a wife, not unlike Ellen, older, less charming, plainer, but a sympathetic companion who would understand him and love him. He too might have had naughty, willful, but very dear and engaging children.

At last an evening came which was pleasanter than all the others. It chanced one morning that Mrs. Wentworth proposed to her brother-in-law that he and Ellen and some of the children should have an early lunch, and then drive over to Annersley, a large town ten miles away, where she wanted some important errands done. Mrs. Allen and several New York friends were to come to lunch, and it would be a comfort to be freed from some of the turbulent and omnipresent children. So it happened that a wagonful of happy people drove "over the hills and far away," that August afternoon. Ellen was on the back seat with Marion and Carlotta, while Beatrice and Bobby proudly shared the front seat with their uncle Maurice. Unhappily, the carriage was not sufficiently elastic to hold all the children, and poor Hester had the doubtful reward of the good, and was left behind because she was no trouble to her mother, while Eleanor was compelled to stay at home because she was so very young.

They drove through patches of dense woods and up long stretches of dusty road, with a tangle of blackberry bushes and early goldenrod on either side of the rough stone walls. Sometimes they passed deserted farmhouses with their blinds forlornly closed, and again they went by prosperous farms that had been reclaimed by summer visitors; and all the way was brightened by a summer sun, except when the sun was obscured by summer clouds. Once they came suddenly, after a bend in the road, upon an old farmhouse, unpainted, and turned by stress of weather to a picturesque gray. Over its walls gay morning-glories were climbing, and in its straggling, unkempt garden was a profusion of hollyhocks; while on the very upper edge of the hillside, silhouetted against the sky, was a flock of white geese.

"That is like one of Vedder's pictures," said Maurice.

"What! those ugly geese, craning their necks in that stupid way?" asked Beatrice.

"You are a true child of your father," he rejoined.

"Does n't papa like geese, uncle Maurice?"

"No, my dear, he does not."

A FAITHFUL FAILURE

But if his niece was unsympathetic, no shade of the picturesque landscape was lost upon Ellen. On this enchanting afternoon, even prosaic errands in ugly Annersley caught a little of the glamour that enveloped everything. Ellen lingered unnecessarily in the shops from a willful determination to make this happy day last a brief hour longer. She hailed with pleasure Beatrice's proposition that they should get soda water at the corner drug store, where their uncle Maurice treated them all, from Beatrice, who with difficulty could be dissuaded from having sarsaparilla, vanilla, and chocolate mixed, down to the small Carlotta. Ellen lavishly provided them with crackers, peppermint drops, and gum drops. When they started to drive home at last, and saw that the summer clouds were fast getting the better of the summer sun, Ellen recklessly hoped that they might be caught in a drenching rain, and have to take refuge in the weather-beaten farmhouse. It was such a humble wish that it was granted her by fate. The shower was upon them almost before they knew it, and Maurice

A FAITHFUL FAILURE

had just time to get the open wagon under shelter of the barn that was near the farmhouse, when the clouds descended in a blinding sheet of rain. It was five o'clock already, and there were eight miles still before them to travel.

"Uncle Maurice," said Beatrice, as she climbed up into the hayloft, "would n't it be jolly fun if we had to stay here all night?"

"I wish it would rain, and rain, and rain, for forty days and forty nights, and that we could have this barn for our ark," added the more imaginative Carlotta.

As the minutes passed, it became evident that a fraction of this wish was to be fulfilled, and Maurice presently proposed that they should adjourn to the farmhouse, and seek shelter there for the night. They were greeted at the kitchen door by the farmer's wife, a cheery, elderly woman.

"Come right in and make yourselves to home," she said hospitably, before Maurice had finished accounting for their sudden appearance.

"I am Maurice Wentworth, from the

Wentworth farm," he said, raising his voice, for the woman was deaf.

"Du tell! I want ter know! I've often seen the farm as I've drove by. And so these are your children?" (she included Ellen in the number) — "four girls and a boy; quite a little family. I guess the boy is a prime favorite with his pa?"

"He isn't our father; he is our uncle Maurice," Bobby and Beatrice explained. But the woman did not hear them, and proceeded to open the parlor door with a flourish.

"Walk right in, girls; don't be bashful. You and your sisters can have the spare room upstairs," she said, addressing Ellen, "and I have a nice little corner room for your father and brother."

"He isn't her father, and she isn't my sister. She's our aunt Ellen, and he's our uncle Maurice," said Bobby.

"I'll get tea for you directly," the woman continued, "for I know little folks is always hungry, and maybe your father" —

"He is *not* our father; he is our uncle Maurice!" shouted the children.

A FAITHFUL FAILURE

"I want ter know! Well, your uncle, maybe, will like a bit of steak."

Before Maurice would have his supper, he insisted upon driving back to Annersley to let Charlotte and Robert know by telephone the whereabouts of their children.

"It's no use going out again in this dreadful rain," said Beatrice, "for papa and mamma never worry about us. They 'll know we are safe somewhere."

Maurice, however, was not to be dissuaded from his purpose, but took the solitary drive in the teeth of the storm.

When he returned, Ellen met him in the entry. "How wet you are!" she said. "I am very sorry! The children were so hungry that I let them have their supper, but I have waited for you. I hope Robert was properly grateful!"

"Grateful!" exclaimed Maurice, with a little laugh. "When I told him that you and the children were safe at Farmer Brown's, and that we were going to spend the night there, he said, 'Hang it, Maurice, did you drive all the way back to Annersley to tell me that? I did n't suppose you were picnicking in the middle of the road.' And then I heard him say to some one near at hand, presumably Charlotte, 'What a fool my brother Maurice is!'" He suppressed the epithet which had accompanied the words.

"How unkind of him!" exclaimed Ellen indignantly.

"Oh, no," Maurice returned dispassionately, as he divested himself of his dripping overcoat. "After an acquaintance of nearly forty years with his brother Maurice, I have come to the conclusion that Robert is about right."

To take supper in the old-fashioned kitchen, with Ellen at the other end of the table, pouring out tea for him, and a little boy and three small girls for his butler and maids, was a new experience for Maurice, but one that was still more delightful was in store for him. When Ellen started to go upstairs to put the children to bed, she was uncertain as to whether she ought to come down again. Anything so charming as a whole evening alone with Mr. Wentworth her New England conscience viewed with doubt. Mrs. Brown helped to dissipate her scruples

A FAITHFUL FAILURE

when she opened the door into the parlor and said, "I hope you and your father — Lord! I forget that he is your uncle — well, I hope you and your uncle will make yourselves entirely to home."

"I shall see you again, Ellen?" Maurice said, as he bade the children goodnight.

"I was just wondering whether it was worth while to come down," she replied, with hesitation.

"Worth while?" His face clouded with disappointment. "That is for you to judge. But I will promise not to make you talk if you wish to be silent," he went on, wholly misunderstanding her. "I will read to you whatever you like."

When she came downstairs, half an hour later, Maurice was obliged to retract this statement. "I made a rash promise," he remarked. "I can't read whatever you like, Ellen, for Mrs. Brown's library consists of but three volumes. Which shall it be? A chapter from the Bible, extracts from Pilgrim's Progress, or a play of Shakespeare's?" He held the bulky Shakespeare in his hand as he spoke.

A FAITHFUL FAILURE

"I won't disappoint you by insisting on The Pilgrim's Progress," she answered, with a smile. "Let it be one of Shakespeare's plays."

"Which one? You shall choose your favorite."

"If it is to be my favorite play, it will be Romeo and Juliet."

"Good heavens, child! not that ghastly tragedy! Ellen, you show how young you are by making such a choice. Let me read As You Like It."

"The tragedies are so much more romantic," observed Ellen.

"And you really prefer tragedy to mirth-provoking humor?"

"Yes. Humor is so commonplace. Besides, I can't help going on with the plays, and thinking of the matter-of-fact lives that the heroes and heroines lived afterwards. I am sure Orlando scolded Rosalind when his beefsteak was not cooked to a turn, and that he held her responsible for all the faults of their children. I shall never forget the wild state your brother was in when my sister was making up her mind whether she would marry him. And look how comfortably prosaic they are now; how he criticises her gowns, and how he finds fault every morning with the coffee!"

"And how he loves her!" added Maurice. "I can hardly imagine his life apart from hers."

"But the romance is gone," persisted Ellen. "Now with Romeo and Juliet everything is so complete!"

"I suppose you will despise me, Ellen, as an old fellow without any sentiment, when I tell you that my ideal of happiness is a handsome house with all the modern improvements, and a wife, who may be plain and unamiable, but who must know how to make me comfortable!"

"Mr. Wentworth!"

"I have not knocked about the world for fifteen years without having gained a realizing sense of the importance of good, matter-of-fact, unromantic prose. Give me a creature not too bright and good to *cook* human nature's daily food!"

"Mr. Wentworth, I know you are not in earnest. I have always supposed you were too " — she hesitated — " I have al-

A FAITHFUL FAILURE

ways supposed you were indifferent to such things."

"Then you have supposed wrong. It is not the men who have had poor coffee all their lives who are indifferent to good coffee."

Ellen laughed.

"It is not the men who have been unprosperous all their lives who are indifferent to prosperity," he went on more seriously.

"Why have you been unprosperous?" she asked impulsively.

"Ah! 'That is another story,' as Kipling would say. It is not a tragedy exactly after Shakespeare's manner, and yet it is not a comedy."

"Tell me all about your life, from beginning to end," she entreated.

"It is not an interesting story, Ellen; and you, with your love of romance, will be disturbed because it is not more complete. To finish it off neatly, I ought to have died half a dozen years ago."

"Oh, no," she said, with a little shiver. "Please go on," she added, after a moment of silence.

"It is a story briefly told. I have failed at everything, and when I had the typhoid fever, six years ago, I even failed to die."

"Were you very ill?"

"Yes. I had as narrow a squeak as any man ever has who lives. Forgive me, Ellen; 'squeak,' I realize, is not the language of Shakespeare."

"Were you on the ranch when you were ill?" she inquired in a subdued voice.

"Yes. I was alone for days, until a neighbor happened to drive over and found me half unconscious. But here I am, you see," he ended cheerfully, "all ready to read aloud Romeo and Juliet."

"I want to hear everything about yourself first, from the very beginning. Why was it that Robert went to college before you, when you were the older brother?"

"Because he was stronger and brighter and more determined than I. Father could only afford to send one of us; so Robert went, and I stayed at home and earned the money to go later."

"It was selfish of Robert to let you do it!" she cried indignantly.

"No, it was weak of me. If I were to live my life over again, I should fight for my rights at every point."

"You would not be half so nice if you did."

"Thank you, — perhaps not; but I should be a great deal happier."

"Are n't you happy now?" asked Ellen, with a great concern in her brown eyes.

"Just at this moment I am very happy."

"You know I did n't mean that. You ought to be happier than Robert," she proceeded thoughtfully, "for you make everybody happy."

"Well, I am not so happy as Robert, all the same. I would change places with him in a minute, if I had the chance. At least, I would if I could go back a dozen years."

"You would n't change places with him if you could. You would want to keep your individuality."

"Think what he has accomplished," said Maurice, with enthusiasm. "He is not only happy himself, but he has made a great many other people happy."

"Yes. I certainly ought to be grateful to him, for he has supported me ever since I was twelve years old. Only — perhaps I can't explain myself — it sometimes seems to me as if it were better to fail than to succeed. Prosperous people are apt to lose their sympathy for the forlorn and unsuccessful, but those who have not succeeded are in touch with all sorrow and failure and misery; and the unsuccessful class is such a large one that to belong to it implies a freemasonry with nine tenths of the world."

"Ellen, you almost make me determine to go on failing to the end of the chapter."

He saw by the quick change in her responsive face that she was pained because he treated her words lightly. In reality he was not unappreciative. On the contrary, it was because he was afraid of expressing too much that he expressed nothing. He looked at the young girl in her inharmonious surroundings, and the stiff haircloth chair in which she sat and the ugly yellow-and-green sprigged paper on the walls instantly became dear and homelike. Even the scarlet worsted mat under the kerosene lamp was faithfully photographed upon his mental retina. These things were part of an enchanting present which would all too soon be only an enchanting past. Ellen wore the summer uniform of her sex, a plain dark blue serge skirt and a blue silk shirt waist dotted with white, but it seemed to him that she wore them with a grace and distinction that were all her own. He was glad that she was looking away from him, as he could rest his eyes upon her with greater confidence. He would not have altered a detail of her appearance. The soft brown hair coiled in the knot that Robert thought too simple, the complexion which Robert thought too pale, the large dark eyes with the long lashes, the sweet mouth which Robert thought too grave, were all a part of Ellen, and to change a single feature, even to its advantage, would be to make her less completely Ellen. Suppose she were really his daughter, as their hostess had fancied? In this case his life and hers would be inextricably joined. But no, some lover would ruthlessly claim her, — he felt a righteous indignation toward the intruder, — and the next moment his wayward imagination was picturing how it would seem to be Ellen's lover.

"Hear the rain beat against the window!" she said. "It is a fearful night. When I was a little girl I used to be afraid of the wind when it shrieked like that."

"Suppose I read King Lear, since you like tragedy? That play is in harmony with the storm."

"I wish you had your essays here, and then you could read those."

"They are as unsuccessful as the rest of my career. Sometimes the magazines and newspapers take them, but oftener they refuse them. They are not essays, by the way, but merely articles about the woods and fields and the Western country."

"Please give me a little sketch of one."

"Ellen, you are an apt pupil of my brother. Don't start me on that subject, or I shall feel sure that you are taking his advice and trying to draw out a bore."

Whatever her motive might have been, it is certain that she succeeded in making him talk more freely about himself than he had ever done, and the hours sped by only too quickly.

"What time is it?" she asked at last, reluctantly.

He took out his watch. "I would rather not tell you," he owned.

Ellen glanced over his shoulder.

"Eleven o'clock!" she exclaimed in horrified accents. "And I thought it was n't more than half-past nine!"

"Good-night, Ellen."

He clasped her slender hand in his, and wished again that he were her father, that he might claim a father's privilege. In the watches of the night he admitted that he had been dishonest with himself: he did not wish that he were Ellen's father.

That night, as Ellen lay awake, she felt that she had said all she ought not to have said, and left unsaid all that she ought to have said. Why had her tongue refused to translate the message of her heart, and to tell Mr. Wentworth the stimulus that his friendship was to her? Why had she not said: —

"When I was a little girl, you showed me all the treasures of the woods and the fields. You taught me to love nature, and to feel as if nothing really mattered so long as one had God's blue sky overhead and a world of beauty at one's feet. You taught me to care for books, and to feel that one never could be dull or friendless with these good comrades at hand. Robert has given me an outwardly prosperous life, but he would have left my mind cramped. And so, I believe that to fail so far as the world is concerned, but to succeed in making one human being independent of the world, is better than to succeed, as the world calls it, but to fail in regard to spiritual things. 'For is not the life more than meat?'"

Why had she not said this? It was because of her miserable shyness and self-consciousness. Instead of this (oh, mortifying thought! her cheeks burned at the recollection), she had told him that to fail was better than to succeed, thereby imply-

A FAITHFUL FAILURE

ing that his life had been a failure. Why had she not urged him to try for mere material, worldly success, since he craved it? It was because no one had ever really cared for him or believed in his powers that he, with his humble estimate of himself, had failed. A part of this she would get courage to tell him in the morning, for Ellen was still young enough to believe in "tomorrow."

Yet alas! when to-morrow came it brought altered conditions. Poor Ellen could not determine what subtle change had come over Maurice Wentworth, and she was too sensitive and shrinking to force her mood upon him. It was a glorious morning, and there was no excuse for lingering at the Browns' farm after breakfast; and indeed, she no longer cared to linger, for the charm had departed.

When they reached home, and Ellen saw Charlotte standing in the doorway, she felt a premonition that some bad news was in store for her.

"Dear Ellen," her sister said, "I want to prepare you for something very sad."

Ellen's heart sank still lower as a sudden memory of awful sorrow years ago swept over her; then it gave a bound again when she saw Robert, Hester, and Eleanor.

Charlotte held a telegram in her hand. "Aunt Martha has died," she announced. "The funeral is to-morrow. Robert thinks that all three of us had better go down to it, as Maurice can stay with the children. I am so sorry for poor aunt Ellen. How lonely she will be!"

"Yes," said Ellen the younger, "poor, poor aunt Ellen!"

Her mind, however, refused to feel a realizing sense of her aunt's sorrow. She was conscious instead of a passionate regret that this journey was to come now, and lessen her time, already too short, under the same roof with Maurice Wentworth. She was ashamed of her lack of sympathy, and would fain have cried because she had no tears to shed.

Maurice drove them to the station the next day, in the same wagon that had so recently gone on a happier errand, and he watched the train wistfully as it moved out of sight.

A FAITHFUL FAILURE

When the travelers came home, four days later, they found a great fire of fir cones and pine-balsam burning in the parlor fireplace, while the room was decorated with cardinal flowers and goldenrod, in honor of their return.

Bobby flew to greet his papa, while the younger children clung joyfully to their mamma, and Beatrice and Hester put their arms around their aunt.

"It is awfully nice to get you back," said Beatrice.

"Did you have a good time?" asked Hester timidly.

"Hester," Beatrice remarked severely, "people don't have a good time at funerals."

Poor Hester, who had meant to say something quite different, and was more sympathetic in her heart than any of the children, retired, crushed and humiliated, to the other end of the room, where she was joined by her uncle.

"Hester," he began, "I believe you and I are really fonder of your aunt than the other children are, but for that very reason we often fail to say the right thing.

A FAITHFUL FAILURE

Suppose we go now and tell her how sorry we are that she has had this long, sad journey."

He took Hester's hand, alike unconscious of the passionate love and gratitude in the child's heart and of the strong influence he was already exerting over her life, and they crossed the room to where Ellen sat in the window-seat, with Beatrice and Carlotta in their white gowns making a sharp contrast against the sombre folds of her black dress.

"We have come to tell you how glad we are to get you back, and how sorry we are for your sorrow," said Maurice.

Ellen raised her clear eyes to his. It seemed dishonest to let him think she had suffered.

"I never knew aunt Martha well enough to love her," she explained, "and so I did not grieve for myself, but merely kept thinking in a vague, outside way, 'How hard it must be to lose the sister with whom one has lived so many years!' Yet the thought did not touch me. It only saddened me, as one is saddened by sad music, or by the first bleak, gray days of winter. It was a mood, not a reality; yet now I have come away, the mood still stays, and it seems as if I could never be glad any more."

"How funny!" said Beatrice. "I should think the time to be sad was at the funeral, and that you'd be awfully glad now to think it was over. Mamma and papa aren't sad. They are laughing. Goodness! Bobby has put on my shade hat. What a scamp that boy is!" and she slid down from her aunt's lap and proceeded to chastise the erring Bobby.

"Robert was so kind and sympathetic through everything," Ellen said to Maurice. "He is the best fellow in the world when one has a real sorrow. No son could have been kinder than he was to aunt Ellen. He felt her grief much more keenly than I did."

"Perhaps so; yet you will feel it longer."

"I shall have a chance to feel it for a long, long time," said Ellen in a low voice, "for I am going to live with my aunt Ellen."

"Robert," Charlotte asked that night after they had gone upstairs, "has it ever occurred to you that Maurice is in love with Ellen?"

"Great Scott! What put that absurd idea into your head?"

"I have suspected it for some time, but I was sure of it to-night by the way he took the news of her going to live with aunt Ellen. Do you suppose, if you get that position for him at Torrey and Brown's, that he will offer himself to her?"

"Charlotte, the men of our family may be fools, but they are not knaves. We don't marry when we have n't money enough to eke out a decent living."

"But Maurice has always supported himself, after a fashion."

"He has contrived to starve with philosophy, but he is not the man to drag a woman into starvation."

"It seems a pity, Robert, that such a good fellow should be so weak in some ways."

"It is a pity. There is hope for the drunkard, the gambler, or the libertine, for the very qualities that dragged him down may raise him up, if turned to good account; but there is no reforming your conscientious, self-distrustful, and consequently inefficient man. Lord! what a conscience that fellow has! I can't think of any place that he could fill with entire satisfaction to himself, unless it were matron of an Orphans' Home. He never could get rich in any line. He is the kind of man who always puts the largest strawberries in the bottom of the box. He won't make a good salesman if he gets in at Torrey and Brown's, for he will point out to his customers every flaw in each article. By the way, he told me, characteristically, to be sure to tell Torrey and Brown that he had had no experience as a salesman."

"If his eyes were only stronger, he could be editor of some newspaper," Charlotte suggested, "for he is clever with his pen."

"My dear child, he would not stay on the staff of a paper a week, for he would insist upon telling the truth, the whole truth, and nothing but the truth. It is pleasant to look forward to a future world for such men. Maurice is very well fitted for the kingdom of heaven; only he would want to change places with some fellow who was writhing in the other kingdom before he could be quite easy in his mind."

"Robert, what troubles me more than the fact that Maurice is in love with Ellen is the fear that she cares for him. If she had a suspicion of his feelings, I am afraid she would be only too glad to 'starve' with him 'with philosophy.' As she can't go to aunt Ellen for a month, I wish we could send Maurice away now. Couldn't Torrey and Brown make room for him at once?"

"I will write to them this moment and find out. But, my dear, I can't believe that your sister would be such an idiot as to marry a man who could earn perhaps six hundred dollars a year."

"She is a child about money matters, and she will reason that the five thousand dollars aunt Martha left her will give her"—

"Two hundred and fifty dollars a

year," said Robert promptly. "At aunt Ellen's she will have comforts and luxuries, and be the cherished daughter of the house, a much more important person than she could ever be in our large family. She will make a good match in time, when she has learned her own value, for she is a pretty girl, and a sweet-tempered girl, and I suppose, if she lives with your aunt Ellen, she will eventually have all her money. Great Scott! Fancy a girl's throwing away all these chances to live with Maurice Wentworth in an attic!"

"She is young and romantic," said Charlotte, "and she has no conception of the wear and tear of poverty. If we can only get Maurice away at once, however, no great harm will have been done."

"He shall go this week, if I have to drag him away by main force."

Robert, who had never failed in any undertaking, did not fail now, and consequently Maurice found himself, at the end of the week, about to start for New York, to be a clerk in the wholesale firm of Torrey and Brown, at a salary of fifty dollars a month. Small as the sum was, he was afraid it was more than his services were worth. He knew that he ought to be grateful to Robert, instead of feeling a smouldering anger at the irritating way in which the chance was offered him, as if Robert were his master, and he a faithful hound, who was expected to take a cuff without a murmur, because it was accompanied by a bone; he knew that he was in no position to rebel at the distastefulness of the work, and that he ought to be glad it was to begin at once; but every other feeling was merged in blank, dumb despair at the prospect of the immediate parting from Ellen.

Maurice spent his last afternoon on the piazza, with a book in his hand; but his eyes frequently wandered toward the court where Ellen was playing tennis with Frank Allen. The mellow sunlight filtered through the green leaves of the oak-tree and fell on her slender figure in the accustomed blue skirt and silk waist that seemed so much more a part of her than her black dress. As he saw her swiftly sending the balls over the net, with apparently no thought in her mind beyond the game, he felt that she had entered a young world, full of gayety and sunshine, in which he had no part. Only the other day there had seemed so close an affinity between them that he had forgotten the barriers of poverty and age; but now her youth and beauty resumed their old position in his thoughts. At the end of the game the two young people sat down on the bench under the oak-tree, and Maurice saw that Ellen had learned her lesson well, for there was the same expression of attentive gravity on her face which only the other night she had given to himself. A blind feeling of jealousy seized him, as, in fancy, he saw her, in the days to come, surrounded by a throng of young fellows, and won at last by some fortunate man with good looks and wealth for his allies. He had been a fool to think that this friendship was without danger for him. He knew now that he loved her with his whole strength; that in fact he had loved her throughout this brief, bright summer. Perhaps some day he might be grateful for this taste of happiness, but at the moment his heart was full of bitterness against society, and the miserable limitations of his own nature. Why was he doomed to loneliness and failure, when others were blessed with love and with success? Was not his heart overflowing with affection? And could he not make a woman happy?

When Ellen and Frank Allen came up the piazza steps, on their way into the house, Maurice fixed his eyes aggressively on his book. Ellen opened the door into the hall.

"Mr. Allen, you will find my sister inside," she said. "She will amuse you while I go to make myself presentable for tea."

Nevertheless she did not follow him into the house. She came over to the corner where Maurice was sitting. He did not raise his eyes from his book.

"I have come to say my own especial good-by to you now," she began in a low tone, "because when you go away to-night it will be a general good-by."

"What difference does it make when

the good-by is said?" he responded almost roughly.

She turned quickly to hide her tears. She had hoped for something different, for some farewell words of regret that their happy summer was over, perhaps for a request that she would write to him sometimes. In that moment, her past, present, and future came before her with panoramic clearness, and Maurice was everywhere the central figure. She remembered a day of hopeless misery after he had gone away when she was a little girl, and the nights which followed, when she had cried herself to sleep. She recollected how she had waited and watched for a letter, that came at last, for he never disappointed children, although he could be cruel to older people, it seemed. Now her whole life was full of him, when he was present and when he was absent; and he was to be absent again, and perhaps absent always! Well, be it so! And since she was nothing to him, her pride would save her from ever letting him know how weak she had been. He should not claim a fraction of her regard whenever he saw fit to ask for it. She would bid him a final good-by. As she turned towards him he was struck by something in her expression.

"Ellen, you expect to be happy with your aunt Ellen, do you not?" he questioned.

"Yes, but just now I am feeling unhappy at the idea of leaving my sister and the children."

"That is perfectly natural; but you will enjoy life as soon as you get there. They tell me that you are to have more freedom, and that you will know a great many young people; that will be pleasant for you. It is a life much more suited to a girl of your age. You are sure to like it."

Ellen turned her head away again abruptly. "Oh, of course, I shall like it," she said quickly. "Children are always pleased with a new toy." And she went into the house without another word.

"After all, I was mistaken about Ellen," Charlotte said to Robert that night. "It is evident that she **is** not in love with Maurice, for she was so friendly when she bade him good-by. If she cared for him, she would have been colder, **or** else less at her ease. I am glad that **you sent** him away in time."

"Of course she is n't in love with him," her husband returned. "I told you so all along. He is n't the kind of man that girls fancy. Poor fellow! He is destined to be a failure in everything."

THE QUEEN OF CLUBS

THERE are eighteen clubs and classes in Riverside, and my sister Eleanor was asked to join thirteen of them, but compromised on eight. I am glad that I am still a schoolgirl, for I am sure that I should die if I had to go to eight clubs. In addition to these festive gatherings among the rich she spends one evening in the week at a Girls' Club for the poor. I always supposed that one of the advantages of poverty was that you did not have to belong to clubs, but it seems that even the poor cannot escape the weight of their environment.

Eleanor's clubs differ in importance: there is one glory of the sun, and another of the moon, while besides these luminaries there are some small stars and one or two unimportant fireflies. There is in especial a club that meets in Boston every

Saturday morning that might be called the sun.

Well, as I remarked before, I am glad that I am only seventeen. My sister Eleanor is twenty-eight, but nobody would ever imagine it. I am sometimes mistaken for her, which makes me furious; but I ought to feel flattered, I suppose, for she is prettier than I am. Although she is so much quieter than I, she is a great favorite. I should like to be such a favorite, except that it means making one's self agreeable to so many stupid people, and — eight clubs! If I were a man, I should fall in love with Eleanor; not that it would do the smallest good, only I could not help it, for she is so sweet. I know that is what Mr. Morris thinks; and he would agree with me in being certain that it did not do any good. Indeed, I should suppose he would feel that it did a great deal of harm, poor fellow. I am sure that he has been in love with her for six years — ever since she has lived with aunt Esther, in fact; and six years make a great deal of difference, at his age. He never was very young, — that is, since I have known him;

but now he is really old, forty-one, with gray hair, and a face that looks as if it had seen better days. I mean in the way of looks; it could never have been any more amiable than it is now. I know Eleanor would like him if she lived in less of a whirl, but she has not any time to fall in love.

Lord Byron said: —

> "Man's love is of man's life a thing apart,
> 'T is woman's whole existence."

Poor antiquated Lord Byron! It is plain to see that he did not live in the present day in Massachusetts! What time has Eleanor to think of love as she eats a hurried breakfast, and flies — no, not flies, for Eleanor is always dignified, but strolls down town rather fast on a Monday morning, to do her marketing early, so that she may not be late for the Musical Club? That Musical Club is the one thing I envy her, for I can play pretty well, and I have quite a good voice. I am not musical enough for the club, however, for the members have to play and sing uncommonly well, or else not at all. Eleanor neither plays nor sings, but she looks so exquisitely refined and so pretty in her brown hat and gown that she lends distinction to the occasion ; and then she is always delightfully sympathetic. What people want is sympathy. I have come to the conclusion that it is better not to try to accomplish some great work in the world, but simply to go about like my sister Eleanor, sympathizing with the people who do things well. Of course there are plenty of things that she does well, but they are of a domestic nature, — all of them, at least, except whist. Eleanor has gone into whist lately, and she plays a fine game. She belongs to three whist clubs ; two of them meet in the afternoon, and one meets in the evening. The Tuesday afternoon club is very swell, and aunt Esther insists upon her going to it every week, but she can't understand why she wastes her time with the Wednesday club. Eleanor says they play whist better in the Wednesday club, but aunt Esther does not see that this is of any consequence. Eleanor certainly has no time to think of love on Monday, Tuesday, or Wednesday ; and Thursday is equally full ; for there is the Renaissance Club in the afternoon, and the Whist Club in the evening; while on Friday — dear me, I have forgotten what happens on Friday morning, but it is something very important, and then there are the Symphony Rehearsals in the afternoon, and the Girls' Club in the evening; and as for Saturday, it is the busiest day of all. Eleanor leaves home directly after breakfast, and does not appear again until tea-time. I wish it were late dinner, but it is n't, because aunt Esther is so old fashioned; it is only plebeian, unsubstantial, unsatisfactory tea.

When I came to spend the winter here, mamma told me to be sure to keep a journal and record my impressions. She said I must give up being frivolous, and become precisely like a Boston girl. She told me that they were all so intellectual here; but I am sure that Eleanor is n't; she hardly reads at all. She is read to, however, a great deal at her clubs. This saves time, because she does not have to stop to hunt up the books, and it is more sociable. They say in New York that everybody is reading in Boston all the time, in all sorts of odd places, but I have never noticed it, except among the men in the electric cars, and they all read the newspapers diligently, — especially when there are ladies standing. I have discovered why men in other cities are so much more polite about giving up their seats: it is because the cars are not so crowded, and they never have to stand long. There are some men, however, who cheerfully relinquish their seats here, and Edward Morris is one of them. I always come back to him, no matter with what subject I start. He is very nice. I wish he were twenty-one instead of forty-one, and were in love with me. We are excellent friends, and I often think of advising him to offer himself to Eleanor by letter. There is never any time for him to do it in any other way, for on the rare occasions when she is at home the house is filled with people. I believe that if he were to offer himself to her often enough by letter he might make an impression on her after a while, just as an advertisement, which they say nobody sees at first, catches the eye when it has been read several times. He might say: —

"My Dear Eleanor, — Won't you cease to be queen of clubs, and be queen of my heart? Pray listen to me on account of my long suit. It has lasted for six years; and although it is not a suit of diamonds, at least, thank Heaven, it is not a suit of clubs."

If this failed to touch her heart, he could send a Musical Club offer a little later: —

"My dear Eleanor, — The andante movement has been going on for six years. Let us have something a little more rapid. My life has hitherto been in a minor key; won't you henceforth make it in A major?"

If this did not suffice, it could be followed by an offer appropriate to a young woman who founded a club to investigate the Middle Ages and the Renaissance: —

"My dear Eleanor, — I am now in a position thoroughly to understand the middle age; and as you are evidently anxious to learn about that period, I would suggest that instead of going to a club once a week for that purpose, you should study the subject in a tranquil manner at home every day with me. It would truly be a renaissance to me if you would take me, my dear girl."

How could she resist such appeals, especially if they were followed by five other equally appropriate offers?

Poor Mr. Morris is so busy that he does not often get an evening to himself, much less an afternoon; but once in a great while he makes an effort, and comes to see us. Eleanor once told him that she was always at home on Monday, and he said, "If you will tell me when you are not 'at home,' I will come then."

"How flattering!" she retorted, with a little laugh.

"I mean that I would rather come when you are by yourselves, without all the world," he explained.

"All the world does not come on Monday," said Eleanor. "On the contrary, sometimes aunt Esther and I sit here alone the whole afternoon."

In consequence of these encouraging words, he tried it one Monday; but unfortunately, two of the Turners and Fanny Williams and old Mrs. Grant dropped in at the same time. He sat on a small chair, looking very unhappy, and drinking tea out of an eggshell cup because Eleanor had made it, — the tea, I mean. There was a thimbleful of tea in the cup, and also a big lump of sugar which he stirred with a tiny spoon, the right size for a Tom Thumb, and he is so large; he positively seemed like a giant. I could see that aunt Esther was eying her slender, spindle-legged chair with apprehension. All he gained by the call was the pleasure of seeing Eleanor behind a little tea-table, looking awfully pretty in a pink gown while she chatted with Fanny Williams. Eleanor does not talk much, but she listens so intelligently that you always feel as if the conversation had been equally divided. Mr. Morris had a good deal of talk with his cousin, Mrs. Grant; or, to speak accurately, he did a good deal of intelligent listening, and I hope he did not find her such a bore as I do.

When he saw me passing through the hall in my school things he rose with alacrity, for I made a face at him as he sat there looking as if he had lost his last friend.

"Must you leave us so soon?" Eleanor asked him, in surprise.

"Yes, I am going to take a little walk with your sister."

"I know that it was very wrong of me to make up that face," I said, as we set off together, "but next year I shall be grown up and can't do such things, so I must make the most of my time."

"I suppose you will come out next winter, Julia, and go to parties and clubs like all the rest of the world," he remarked, with a little sigh.

"I am never coming out," I replied. "I am going to stay in always. I shall be at home every day in the week."

"So you think now, — so Eleanor thought once; but the pressure is too strong on you girls."

We had a nice walk, and a long talk about my school and all the girls, and I forgot all about Eleanor and his love for her. He is the kind of person who makes one talk about one's own affairs.

He did not try coming again on Monday, poor man! As ill luck would have it, he selected a Thursday afternoon when the Renaissance Club met at our house. He was shown into the parlor, through some mistake; perhaps the maid thought that he was the lecturer. He was well inside the door before he discovered what was going on, for he is very near-sighted, and then he looked so blank. The ladies were intensely interested; most of them know him a little, and they have been wondering for the last six years whether Eleanor would marry him or not. I am sure they must have thought that the wedding day was set. Eleanor was not in the least embarrassed when she saw him. My sister Eleanor is always perfectly calm, and rather cold.

"I am very glad to see you, Mr. Morris," she said. "I will tell Julia that you are here."

She did not know that I was peeping through the dining-room door.

It happened, therefore, that Mr. Morris

and I had another walk, and he heard more about my school and the Saturday evening dancing class, and he appeared very much interested. Men are so much more sympathetic than women. I suppose it is because nowadays they don't have half so much on their minds.

That evening aunt Esther spoke to me seriously. She said that she did not like the way in which I was devoting myself to Edward Morris, for it seemed disloyal to Eleanor. I laughed at first, and I can't remember all that passed, but she implied, finally, that I was trying to make him fall in love with me for the sake of amusing myself, and she told me he was too good a man for me to make unhappy. I grew very angry at last, and I said, " I am not amusing myself; I can promise you safely that if he asks me to marry him I will do it. I am seventeen and he is forty-one, to be sure, but when I am fifty-seven and he is eighty-one we shall be practically the same age."

It was very silly of me. I don't know what aunt Esther thinks. Sometimes I fancy that she believes I was in earnest.

As for Eleanor, she is more wrapped up in her clubs than ever.

January 9. Mr. Morris came one evening last week, but, unfortunately, he hit upon a night when Eleanor was at the Girls' Club. I advised him to come some Sunday evening, and last night he appeared; but Eleanor was so worn out with the fatigue of the week, joined to the depraved actions of her Sunday-school class, that she had gone to bed early.

January 17. Mr. Morris called again last night. I was determined that he should have a chance to see Eleanor alone, so I brought my German books, and asked aunt Esther if she would not come into the other room and help me with my lesson; but the dear soul proposed a game of whist. Theoretically she realizes that Mr. Morris comes to see Eleanor rather than herself, but practically there is never any especial occasion when it occurs to her to leave them to themselves. She says that it is a good thing for a man to see a girl in her home, with her family about her; but I think that it is pleasanter for the family than for the man and the girl.

Aunt Esther delights in whist, but she does not play the modern game. She always tells her partner, with one of her pleasant smiles, that she has never learned how to make trump signals, and that she has played all her life and has found it to her advantage to lead from her short suit. I like that kind of game, and as Eleanor and Mr. Morris prefer science, I proposed that she should play with me; but she said she would rather have Edward Morris for a partner, as in that case she would be more likely to beat. Aunt Esther was especially trying last night. It took her a long time to decide what to play. She has been taking lessons in the Delsarte system, and has learned how to relax; and once when she was particularly long, I could not help saying that I was afraid Eleanor and Mr. Morris did not like relaxed whist.

Life is an odd mixture, and most of it is a great deal duller than novels lead one to expect, as I am sure Mr. Morris must have thought as he sat there all the evening opposite placid, aggravating aunt Esther. Life is very like the Saturday evening dancing class. There is a good deal of sitting around and waiting; there are a few adorable turns and a kaleidoscopic change of partners, then — silence! The evening is over, and the lights are put out. Life is n't very serious, at least in the nineteenth century in Boston, but it is rather amusing, and I suppose we should all miss the hurry, the rush, and the mad dance.

January 21. How lightly I wrote only four nights ago! A terrible thing has happened that has changed the whole world. How could I ever have thought that life was anything but solemn and serious and awful?

I will begin at the beginning, and write it all out just as it occurred. Thursday evening Mrs. Emery sent over to say that she was in dire need of a substitute at her whist club, and to ask if Eleanor would bring me. Poor woman, she must have been in sore distress indeed before she sent for me! Eleanor arranged that I should be her partner. The dear girl hates to play with me, but she dislikes still more to inflict me on any one else. I was frightened at the idea of playing in a whist club, so of course I made more mistakes than ever. Eleanor did not scold me, — she never scolds, — but she grew a little stiffer and a shade quieter. It appeared at the moment as if her whole mind and heart and soul were set upon winning that especial rubber of whist. I wanted to laugh, as I looked around the room and saw the intense, anxious faces. There was no " relaxed whist " that night.

I don't remember how long we had been playing, when the maid came and whispered something into Dr. Emery's ear. He rose quickly and left the room. He was followed by his wife and Mr. Remington. Mrs. Emery came back directly.

"There has been an accident," she said. "A man has been run over by one of those terrible electric cars. I can never get used to them; they seem to me like steam engines let loose."

We stopped for a few minutes to discuss the accident; but whist is whist, and a game in the hand is worth more than an unknown man under the wheel.

"Probably he is an Irishman, and I have no doubt that he had been drinking," said Mrs. Emery.

We all accepted this comfortable theory, and those of us who were not playing at Dr. Emery's table were soon once more cheerfully absorbed.

At the end of half an hour Mr. Remington returned. I heard a whispered consultation between him and Mrs. Emery, and caught the words, "You had better not tell her." I also overheard Edward Morris's name.

The room swam before my eyes, and I caught at the table to prevent myself from falling. I lost all presence of mind.

"Is Mr. Morris dead?" I gasped.

"No, dear; no, indeed," Mrs. Emery answered in a soothing tone. "There is no danger, we trust; but he has met with severe injuries, and my husband has gone with him to the hospital."

It was singular what a difference it made in our feelings when we found that the man who had been run over was not a stranger. Everybody was so sorry and so sympathetic; every one, at least, except Eleanor. She sat there as rigid as a statue, looking as if she wished all this commotion were over, so that she might finish her game. I could have killed her,—I really could, if the ace of clubs in my hand had been the implement of that name instead of a bit of pasteboard. I could see that all the ladies in the room were looking stealthily at her, and then at me. She could see it, too. She drew herself up a little straighter, if that were possible, and said, "Julia, you must control yourself; everything is being done for Mr. Morris that can be done; you must not spoil the evening. Spades are trumps, I believe."

I am sure they all knew then that she was not engaged to Edward Morris.

I tried to play. I tried to keep back my tears, but a few would fall on the ace of clubs, and I ended by putting the hateful thing on Eleanor's king.

"I had taken that trick," she said quietly.

"I don't care if you had!" I burst out.

"I don't care anything about this wretched game. I want to go home. I am very unhappy; please, please let me go home."

Eleanor rose. "I hope you will excuse us, Mrs. Emery," she said. "Pray do not let us break up your evening, but I think that I had better take my sister home. She and Mr. Morris are old friends, and she feels this very much."

Mr. Remington telephoned for our carriage, and he also telephoned to the hospital to learn the latest news concerning Mr. Morris. It seemed that he had reached his destination safely, but was unconscious; and although his life was in no immediate danger, he would probably have a long, serious illness. We all recognized the reserved nature of the message "in no immediate danger," and our hearts sank.

Eleanor was very gentle with me. She did not reprove me for my outburst, and after we were in the carriage she took my hand in hers, but I snatched it away.

"Don't touch me!" I cried fiercely. "You are as cold and hard as a stone. You ought to love him with your whole heart, but you have no heart, and you leave it to me to grieve for him; to me, when I am only the least of his friends."

Eleanor said nothing.

"I am sure that you are responsible for this accident," I went on, rendered quite beside myself by her calmness. "He was thinking of you when his foot slipped. If you had been a little good to him, instead of trying to help a lot of people in clubs, it would not have happened. And perhaps you have killed him," I added.

"Don't, Julia," she said, with a little shudder.

At this point I began to cry, and I sobbed all the way home as if my heart would break.

Aunt Esther met us at the door with a surprised but an approving face.

"How early you are!" she exclaimed. "This is a sensible hour. Edward Morris was here this evening, Eleanor, and he seemed quite hurt when he did not find you. He said he had written to tell you that he was coming."

"I never got the note," Eleanor replied.

"No, it came at noon, and I put it on the mantelpiece in the library with your other letters, and I did not remember to give them to you; for you were at home only long enough to take your tea and dress for the club." Aunt Esther handed her the letters, and Eleanor took them and started to go upstairs.

"I am tired," she said, "and so I will bid you good-night. Julia, you must tell aunt Esther why we came home early."

"I hope you were not badly beaten," aunt Esther observed.

"Beaten?" Eleanor repeated vaguely, with a curious, absent look on her face. "Oh, in whist? No, thank you; at least I don't remember. I think — I think I will say good-night."

I told aunt Esther the news, and then I hurried upstairs; but quick as I was, Eleanor had already locked the door between her room and mine. I knocked, but had no response. I knocked again, and again there was no answer. I paused and listened. There was a faint, muffled sound on the other side of the door. I knew then that Eleanor was crying, and the fact awed me, for I could not remember having heard her cry since father died, six years ago.

"Eleanor, let me in," I begged. "I understand it all now, dear. Please forgive me, and please, please let me in."

But Eleanor would not open the door.

I was so wretched that I was sure I should stay awake all night; for how could I sleep until she had forgiven me? And then I fell asleep while I was thinking it over, miserable, faithless wretch that I was!

In the morning I awoke earlier than usual. The door was open between Eleanor's room and mine, and everything looked so pleasantly familiar that my first feeling was, what it always is, joy that I was in this happy world. Then I remembered that perhaps there would never be any joy for us again.

I went softly into Eleanor's room. She was lying on the sofa, with her wrapper on, and a letter tightly clasped in her hand. Her face was so pale that I was frightened at first, and thought she had fainted; but I soon found she had fallen asleep after a long, anxious night. How long and how anxious it had been I could only faintly fancy, for a glance at her face made me conscious that my sorrow was a childish feeling compared with hers.

While I was standing by her, Eleanor opened her eyes. I shall never forget the look on her face when she tried to smile as if nothing had happened.

"We shall hear some good news to-day, dear," she began; then her lip trembled, and then — it was she who was sobbing, with her head on my shoulder and my arms around her neck.

"Julia, he does love me," said she.

"You need not tell me that when I have known it for six years."

"I did not know it, and I don't think he knew it until lately, but" — She held up the letter by way of an ending to her sentence. I could not help seeing the first words.

"'My dear Queen of Clubs,'" I read aloud, half unconsciously.

Eleanor covered the precious document with her hand, and we both laughed forlornly. "Eleanor, how could you be so calm when you heard the news of the accident?" I asked impetuously.

"Would you have had me show all those people what I felt, when I did not know that he cared for me?" she demanded.

"If you did not know that he loved you, you were a very stupid person."

"We were always good friends," said Eleanor, "and my life was such a full one that until lately I never felt the need of anything else; and then — then — I thought he was in love with you."

"With me?" I said scornfully.

"Julia dear," she began eagerly, "I hope — I hope" —

At last I comprehended everything.

"Yes, I love him," I said firmly. "I love him like a brother, like a father, — like a grandfather, if you will. Darling, does that make you jealous? Are n't you willing that I should love him like a grandfather, Eleanor dear?"

The next morning aunt Esther and Eleanor went to the hospital, but they returned with sad faces. Edward Morris was still unconscious.

January 24. We have had a terrible week. Mr. Morris has concussion of the brain, and his recovery is doubtful. Eleanor has abandoned all her clubs, and does not seem to care any longer what people think, but she is very quiet and calm.

February 3. I am used to Mr. Morris's illness now, for everything is so exactly the same at school and at dancing school. I should die if I were as unhappy all the time as I was that first night; so I try to think that he is going to get well, and to forget Eleanor's sad face.

February 12. The doctor is afraid that Edward Morris will not live many days. This is frightful — though it is possible that he may linger for weeks, or even months. I cannot grasp the idea of his dying. It seems impossible that he can go away from us altogether. In the beginning I realized all the possibilities, but now that we have had this respite I can't believe that anything so overpoweringly sad will happen; and after all, there is still a faint chance that he may rally.

Mrs. Grant is going to have the whist club just the same, even though she is his cousin. She says that one can't give up everything for an indefinite period on an uncertainty. I believe that they would play whist on the edge of his grave, — all except Eleanor; she does not play any more. She and aunt Esther go in every day to the hospital to see if there is anything that they can do, but Mr. Morris does not know them. Poor Eleanor! she realizes the situation only too well.

February 23. I am so happy that there are no words in the English language to tell my delight. Edward Morris is out of danger. He will be an invalid for a year or two, as he will not be able to use his brain much for a long time; but Edward Morris without a head is so much nicer than any other man with one that it does not matter, and — he is going to get well!!!!! I have put all those exclamation points in a row to help faintly to express my feelings. They stand for joy, rapture, happiness, and every other blissful thing.

Eleanor is perfectly calm, as usual, but the whole expression of her face has changed, and she looks absolutely seraphic.

Edward knew her yesterday; and when she came home I could see that something unusual had happened.

"It is all right, Julia," she replied to my eager questions.

"What did he say, dear?" I asked. "How did he look? What did you say? Tell me all about it."

"I cannot tell you what we said, but we have explained everything."

"Can't you tell me just one little thing?" I pleaded.

Eleanor began to laugh softly. "He said something when I first came in which will amuse you, Julia. He asked what day it was. 'Saturday,' I replied. 'Saturday? Eleanor, how good you were to come here instead of going to the Saturday Morning Club!'"

THE FATTED CALF

LOUISE HENDERSON was sitting in the sewing-room of her uncle's parsonage, with her eyes fastened upon a small blue garment in her lap. There was a look of quiet but intense happiness in her face. This beatific expression could not have been caused by the skirt which she was mending — even her aunt, who was not an observing woman, drew that conclusion — for the tear was a large and irregular one.

"Louise," she asked, "whom is your letter from?"

Louise colored and handed the note to her aunt.

"It is from a young man I met at cousin Susan's — Mr. Matthews. He used to know you; he is going to the White Mountains some time soon, and would like to stay over a train to see you and uncle Henry."

THE FATTED CALF

"Used to know me! I should think so! Ralph Matthews! and I suppose he is entirely grown up now. How time does fly!"

"He is pretty old; he is twenty-nine."

"Of course he is; he is nine years younger than I am. I was seventeen when I went to live at his father's house with mamma, and his father was thirty-seven. Who would have supposed that a sensible man like Hugh Matthews would have fallen in love with a mere child like myself? It was my first love affair."

Louise, who was eighteen, wondered if a disposition to fall in love with mere children ran in the family; then, being a young woman of practical good sense, she took herself to task sharply. "How ridiculous I am to expect anything!" she thought. "Cousin Susan said he was something of a flirt, and I mustn't — and he didn't" —

"When is the young man coming?" inquired her aunt. "Some time this week or next," she added, as she glanced at the note again. "How indefinite! So thoughtless! Men are all the same; they never consider washing days and ironing days, or think that their coming need make any difference; whereas it makes the greatest difference. We must 'kill the fatted calf' for him, not that he is a prodigal, but it is so long since I have seen the dear boy — twenty years — and he is used to having everything in such style. Supposing he should drop down upon us when we have stew for dinner! I do hope the children will behave well. If we only knew when he was coming! My dear, we must have a fresh roast or chickens every day, and then whenever he appears we shall be prepared for him. It will be expensive, but we can economize afterward."

They had a company dinner all that week and the next. The children thought this a delightful plan. They hoped Mr. Matthews would never come, that they might "dine on like this forever."

When two weeks had passed without bringing the expected guest, both aunt and niece gave him up reluctantly, and went back to their former manner of living. There was more to be done than usual, for they had put off giving the parlor a thorough sweeping for a fortnight, lest he should arrive while they were in the midst of it.

On Friday, therefore, the usual day for sweeping, they moved everything out of the parlor into the entry. It was a warm day. The air came in through the hall door enticingly, bringing with it the odor of newly mown hay. The haymakers were at work in the meadow. Louise, wholly enveloped in a blue and white checked apron, and with a sweeping-cap on her pretty brown hair, was patiently dusting all the irregular corners of a carved oak chair. Whenever sweeping day came she wished the family did not have so much old-fashioned furniture. Nora, the maid of all work, was beating the rugs viciously, as if she had some peculiar spite against them. The rugs were out on the grass in front of the house. There was only a strip of some fifty feet of level lawn between the house and the street, so that every one who passed could see all that was going on; but it did not matter, for they would have

THE FATTED CALF

known what was going on, at any rate; they always did in East Bradfield. Louise was still at work on the carved chair, with her back to the street, when she was startled by an exclamation from Nora.

"What is it?" she asked.

"It's the fatted calf, miss, as sure as me name is Nora O'Connor, a-walkin' up the street, just as unconsarned as if it warn't Friday, and a salt-fish dinner a-cookin'!"

"Nora!"

"It's the city chap, sure as I'm born. Turn round and see for yourself, Miss Louise."

Louise looked. She meant to escape afterward, but destiny was stronger than she. Ralph Matthews was just turning in at the gate, and met her confused glance. He had a pleasant face, with a brown beard, and humorous brown eyes which seemed to take in everything. His manner was so polite that it struck her as sarcastic. His faultless attire forced her own deficiencies still more strongly upon her, and made her shy and constrained.

"My aunt is lying down," she said; "I

will tell her you are here. I cannot take you into the parlor for obvious reasons. My uncle is writing his sermon in the study. There is the dining-room," she continued meditatively, "but the children are painting there."

"May n't I stay and help dust the furniture?" he inquired, seating himself tranquilly on the piano stool.

"Louise," called her aunt anxiously, at the head of the stairs, "Tommy has just had a frightful bump on his forehead. Could you — Why, Mr. Matthews! I know it must be Mr. Matthews, for you look so much like your poor dear father. *How* do you do? Louise, take him into the study directly. How could you be so thoughtless as to let him stay here?" and she descended the stairs full of apologies.

Mrs. Henderson took possession of her old acquaintance willy-nilly, and carried him off to the study. "Henry," she said, "here is a dear old friend of mine — Ralph Matthews. It was so kind of him to come to this out-of-the-way spot to see me again."

Mr. Henderson looked up from his sermon with the dazed air of a man who is in the full swing of inspiration. For a moment he hovered helplessly between two worlds, the next he descended regretfully to this one. "I am glad to see you," he said, taking off his old-sighted glasses. He had charming manners as soon as he had recovered himself; their gentleness was a distinction in itself, and assorted well with his gray hair and fine blue eyes.

"I am delighted to see you," young Matthews returned cordially.

Mr. Henderson gave one more regretful look at his sermon, the sheets of which were spread about in confusion on his table, together with a pile of unanswered letters. Books were there too, — both opened and unopened; in fact, there were books in every available nook in the room. The very windows seemed an impertinent interruption, for both the space above and below them was utilized by book shelves.

"I am interrupting you," Ralph Matthews said. "Miss Henderson will take good care of me, I know, until you are at leisure."

"No," protested Mrs. Henderson; "you must stay here at present, for Louise and I are such *busy* people. Mr. Henderson will work all the better afterward for a little rest."

"Louise," she said, when she rejoined her niece, "it is quarter past twelve. We shall have to put dinner off until two o'clock, and suppress the salt fish; it is too countrified. You will have to run downtown and get some steak or chops. Chops breaded, with tomato sauce, will be the best. We have n't a can of tomatoes in the house. If they can't send the things up directly, you must bring them; and get a bottle of salad oil too; we used the last on Saturday, when I was so sure Mr. Matthews would come."

Louise slowly divested herself of her apron and sweeping-cap, and went to the closet for her hat.

"Get a head of lettuce too," said her aunt — "two heads if they are small. You will have plenty of time to make a salad dressing. We shall need two cans

THE FATTED CALF

of tomatoes; we will have mock bisque soup. It is a mercy one can always fall back upon that in an emergency."

Louise put on her broad-brimmed hat, trimmed with white mull.

"Will you take Polly with you?" called her aunt. "She is so fretful, and she will be company for you, and I have my hands full with Tommy; poor boy, I had forgotten all about his bump."

Little four-year-old Polly clung delightedly to her cousin's hand, and the two stepped out into the fragrant sunshine. Visions of another companion, and a walk in the woods beyond the meadows, had been hovering vaguely in Louise's mind, but she resigned herself cheerfully to the inevitable, as was her habit. Polly walked slowly, and the way was long. She wanted a "drink of water" so persistently that they stopped at last at a neighbor's to get it. Then she wanted another, because that other "drink of water" was so good that it made her more thirsty.

When they started to go home she was made proud and happy by being allowed

THE FATTED CALF

to carry one of the cans of tomatoes. She dropped it only three times on the way back. They met several of the neighbors, who all knew that Mr. Matthews had arrived, and sympathized with Louise.

"To think that he should have come on a Friday!" exclaimed Mrs. Osgood. "I will send you over some of my orange cake; I made it yesterday; and we have plenty of cream, if your aunt would like some."

Mrs. Trumbull offered to exchange her roast of beef for the salt fish.

"You are very kind," said Louise, "but I have some chops here in this bundle, and there is time to cook them."

Louise was so heated by her walk that a cool seat in the china closet, with the salad dressing for a companion, was luxury in comparison.

Johnny came presently and looked in at the window. He had been hindering the men in the hayfield all the morning, under the impression that he was helping them. "Hullo!" he cried; "what are you doing?"

"Making a salad dressing."

"What for?"

"Because Mr. Matthews is going to be here to dinner."

"The F. C.?"

"Don't call names, Johnny."

"I suppose you aren't going to have salt fish for dinner?"

"No."

"How bully! Wish he'd come every Friday."

"I don't."

"I say, cousin Louise," Johnny asked persuasively, "could you mend a fellow's jacket? I tore it on the hay cart."

"I can't possibly mend it."

"But it's mostly all hole. I'm afraid the F. C. wouldn't approve of it."

"Put on your other jacket, then."

"You forget, cousin Louise, the other one has gone up the spout."

"Go to bed, then," she said desperately.

"But, cousin Louise, I want to see the F. C. Please, please do mend my jacket."

"I will, if I have time, Johnny," his cousin returned patiently. She had time;

THE FATTED CALF

she always did have time for everything, and as a reward she was given more and more of the work of the household. She did not mind generally, for she was young and strong and very fond of the children, who thought her a "trump," only she had wistfully hoped that she might have a holiday when Ralph Matthews came to East Bradfield. However, it did not matter, she said to herself, as he had evidently come to see her uncle and aunt. She repeated this phrase over and over to herself throughout dinner. He was placed at her aunt's right hand, and she was on the opposite side of the table.

The children were very good throughout the first course. They were awed by the presence of the stranger, who, however, talked so charmingly that by the second course they found there was nothing awe-inspiring in him, after all. Consequently they grew confidential.

"We don't have chops and tomato sauce every Friday," Grace remarked sweetly.

"Grace, you must n't say such things," said her sister Susie in a loud whisper.

"We're going to have salad presently," Johnny added. "I'm real glad you came," he continued sociably. "I asked cousin Louise if she didn't wish you'd come every Friday, and she said 'no.'"

"Johnny," said his mother, in horrified accents, "you must not tell such stories."

"But it isn't a story; it's true. Ask cousin Louise. I suppose it's because she had so much trouble making the salad dressing."

Poor Louise was the color of a peony. She was too disturbed to laugh, and could not even speak; her tongue seemed to cleave to the roof of her mouth. There was an awful pause for a moment.

Mr. Matthews broke it at last. "You were speaking of the village mir in Russia," he observed, turning to his host; "it is curious the way in which that relic of the Middle Ages has survived all these years."

"How clever he is!" thought Louise, who had never heard of the village mir in Russia; "and how eloquent and eager he has made my uncle! He has the power of drawing every one out. I was a fool to fancy he liked me particularly. He could never care for such an ignoramus, and it is just as well that he should see me in my true colors now."

Louise's aunt sat erect at the head of the table, serene in the consciousness that her dinner was most appetizing. It was unfortunate that the children should have made those malapropos remarks; but at least Mr. Matthews would see that if they did not have such dainty meals every day, they knew how things should be done. The bisque soup was delicious, the chops cooked to a turn, and the salad a dream of delight. There was a long pause after this course, during which Mrs. Henderson nervously wondered what had happened to Mrs. Osgood's orange cake, and whether Nora was waiting to pick the raspberries.

At last the recreant maid appeared, bearing a huge pie, which she placed solemnly before her mistress, who looked at it in speechless wonder. Where did it come from, and what were its contents? Could anything show greater vulgarity of

THE FATTED CALF

breeding than this unexpected but all too substantial apparition? Before she had recovered from her surprise, Nora placed a large ham in front of Mr. Henderson. It was all clear to poor Mrs. Henderson now. The neighbors, in the kindness of their hearts, had sent over these supplements to the feast, and Nora, knowing that her mistress was ambitious to have many courses, had brought them in on her own responsibility.

Mrs. Henderson, who never was able to turn things off with a joke, asked her guest if he would have some meat pie, with the feelings of a criminal at the stake.

"It's veal pie," cried Tommy. "We've killed the fatted calf sure this time."

To add to her confusion, her husband glanced across at her, and said, "Did you mean to have this ham cut, Mary?"

After they had partaken of the raspberries and coffee, Mrs. Henderson was about to rise from the table, when Nora came to her with a warning shake of the head.

"Not yet," she said in a loud whisper;

"there's two more courses a-settin' in the pantry."

"Oh, golly! Let's have 'em both," cried Johnny.

Mrs. Henderson ignored the observations of her maid and her son. She drew her small figure up to its full height, and looked almost majestic.

"I think perhaps we shall find it pleasanter in the other room," she said, with all the grace and dignity at her command.

"It is four o'clock," said her husband, taking out his watch. "How the afternoon has gone!"

"Only an hour and a half before Mr. Matthews's train leaves," thought Louise.

The Hendersons' parlor, to which they adjourned, was a quaint room, with the atmosphere of a former generation lingering about its carved chairs and claw-footed tables. The green carpet, with its huge bunches of gay flowers, had been somewhat softened by Persian rugs, but the stiff portraits which looked down on one from the walls, and the square six-octaved piano remained uncompromisingly old fashioned. There were vases and bowls of roses on the tables and piano, and a general fragrance as if the room were a rose garden.

Louise ensconced herself on the sofa behind a table, with a child on either side of her, and, having fortified herself in this impregnable position, she wondered that Ralph Matthews did not come and talk to her.

"Louise," said her aunt at last, "I wish you would sing something."

"Yes," assented her uncle; "'Duke Street,' or 'Come, ye disconsolate.'"

"Oh, not hymn tunes on a week day, uncle Henry; I should feel positively sacrilegious."

As Louise struck the first chords of "Ye banks and braes of Bonny Doon," she nervously realized how much the piano was out of tune, and the thin, poor quality of the notes. In the presence of this stranger, who lived on terms of intimacy with grand pianos, her much-loved instrument shrank into insignificance.

She did not know how charming she looked in her lilac gown, with the huge bowl of white roses at her right, and the light from the window at her left faintly struggling through the half-closed blinds. Everything was complete about Louise, from her pretty head, with its smooth brown hair, to her trim little figure in the simple but scrupulously neat dress. There were many girls far more beautiful than she, but of her kind she was perfect, and one no more thought of finding fault with her lack of color, or with the shape of her mouth, than of quarreling with the violet for being of a different color and shape from the rose. One might prefer roses, but that was a different matter.

"Now surely, surely he will come to the piano and turn my music for me," she thought.

At this moment a stout person of forty or thereabouts, dressed in an attempt at a tea gown of variegated colors, and adorned with scarlet bows, came into the room, bristling with self-importance. She was introduced to Mr. Matthews as Miss Wiley.

"I have come to play some duets with you, Louise love, as soon as I can recover my breath," she announced. She seated herself in a rocking-chair, and rocked back and forth vigorously, plying a fan with energy.

"Miss Wiley is the organist at our church," Mr. Henderson explained to his guest.

"Are you a musician, Mr. Matthews?" she inquired. "If so, I know you will find these duets very enjoyable. I am trying to inspire my dear Louise with a love for Wagner" (she gave the composer the full benefit of his *W*). "If you was with her long enough, you would find she has not yet a feelin' sense of the scope, aim, and rhythmic beauty of that 'great master of the music of the future.' She came back from New York quite fatigued by him."

Poor Louise! Mr. Matthews had taken her and her cousin to hear Rheingold, and although she had not cared for the music, she had never in all her life passed four happier hours. Would he think she had been bored all that time? She looked at him furtively, but he had turned to speak to her aunt, and did not see her wistful glance. It was hard to have to spend her holiday afternoon in playing duets with Miss Wiley, whom she could barely tolerate at the best of times, and who seemed bent upon proving her intimacy in the household, calling her "dear Louise," and "my sweet friend," as if they were of the same age, and had been playmates from infancy. Miss Wiley always drowned Louise's treble with her bass, but on this particular afternoon she played louder than ever before, as if to impress the Hendersons' guest with a sense of her musical prowess.

At length Louise heard her uncle say in a low tone, "Matthews, if the ladies will excuse us, perhaps you would like to take that walk I told you of, across the meadows to the woods?"

"Perhaps Miss Louise" — she could only distinguish these words in her friend's reply, but they made her heart beat quicker.

"I think not," said her uncle, glancing toward the piano; "she has taken the walk so many times, and it is such a hot day."

THE FATTED CALF

Then Louise took a bold step. She left her companion precipitately in the middle of a duet, and said hurriedly: "I should like very much to go to the woods with you, uncle Henry, if Miss Wiley will excuse me. I want to get some ferns and see the sorrel, if it is out."

"Dear child, we can get the ferns and sorrel for you," said her uncle. "Do not think it necessary to take that long, hot walk just for that."

"I should like to go," she repeated.

"Perhaps Miss Wiley will come too," said her hospitable uncle. By an unusual stroke of luck, however, the cool parlor proved a more alluring place to the organist, who preferred to stay behind with Mrs. Henderson.

As they were all three going out of the gate, Grace and Susie came tearing after them, and begged to be allowed to go too. Their father gave each of them a hand, for which Louise blessed him, and she walked on ahead with Mr. Matthews.

Now that the moment had actually come for which she had longed all day, an access of shyness seized her which made it impossible to frame sentences of more than six words.

"What a charming man your uncle is!" Ralph Matthews began.

"Yes, indeed."

"And this town is such a delightfully quaint, primitive place."

In her present sensitive state of mind these words jarred on her.

"Primitive! How unkind of him!" she thought. "He thinks us primitive because we had veal pie and ham after lettuce. We are primitive because we have a six-octaved piano, and an organist who cannot speak the English language correctly. My uncle is 'primitive,' my aunt is 'primitive,' and I — I am 'primitive.'" She could scarcely keep back the tears. "It is a pretty place," she returned coldly.

"Miss Louise," he began abruptly, "have I offended you in any way?"

"Oh, no."

"You are not as kind to me as you used to be. Is there a reason for it?"

"I am kind enough," said Louise; "but it is such a hot day."

She was as amazed to hear these words as if they had been uttered by another person. They had crossed the road by this time, and were going into the fields behind the Osgoods' house. At this moment Lilian Osgood came out sociably to meet them. She was charmingly pretty, by far the prettiest girl in East Bradfield.

To-day she wore a most becoming white gown. Her yellow hair rippled about her face, and her pink cheeks had the bloom of a peach. Louise thought she looked like a tall white lily. She caught an involuntary expression of admiration on Ralph Matthews's face.

"It is all over with me," she thought.

Of course Lilian would go to walk with them; there was nothing she would like better. She spread her red sunshade, which made her more picturesque than ever, and in another moment Louise found herself with her uncle and the children, while Lilian and Ralph walked off together across the fields, a bright patch of red and white and a dark patch of black against the newly mown grass. Lilian chatted on merrily, and she could hear Ralph laugh from time to time.

"How much he likes her!" she thought. Before they had reached the first stone wall she had pictured the engagement of these two, that she might be prepared for anything, and fortify herself in time; when they entered the woods she had got as far as the wedding; and by the time they had come to the brook she had decided that she would be bridemaid if Lilian asked her, and hold her head so straight and stiff that no one would ever imagine — What? Nonsense! She did not care for Ralph Matthews. She did not like his luxurious life; its forms and ceremonies frightened her. She was hopelessly plebeian, provincial, *primitive*.

The slender, white-stemmed birches, with their pale-green leaves, drooped over the brook, and the solemn pines and hemlocks represented the other extreme in the scale of color. There was every possible gradation of green between the two. The brook hurried on over the impeding stones, breaking into a golden brown in the sunlight, and changing to a deeper brown in

THE FATTED CALF

the shadow, and Louise, who was usually keenly alive to all these things, saw none of them now. Her eyes were fastened on a man with laughing brown eyes, who was talking in an animated manner to a fascinating girl.

Lilian had closed her sunshade, and the light sifted through the trees and shone on her yellow hair. It had evidently caught on some envious branch, for it was all in a pretty fluff, and several charming little curls had escaped their bounds. She was standing helplessly before the log which formed a bridge across the brook, with one foot in its dainty red shoe placed on the edge, while Ralph, with an air of devotion, was holding out his hand and urging her to let him help her.

"How absurd!" thought Louise sharply. "She has a perfectly steady head. She is no more afraid of that log than I am."

When it came her own turn to cross, Ralph was waiting to proffer his services.

"May I help you?" he asked.

"No, thank you," she returned with dignity; "I can get on by myself perfectly well."

So could Grace and Susie. They preferred to go over "all by their own selves."

Louise had waited to urge them to let her carry them across, for their father had stopped to speak to the haymakers. Lilian and Ralph were by this time lost to view in the tangle of underbrush. She walked on slowly, absorbed in her meditations. Suddenly she heard a splash, and turned to see Susie sitting in the middle of the brook with frightened eyes.

"Cousin Louise," she cried, "I'm most dead. Take me out; but the log was so *slippery*."

There was nothing to be done but to get Susie home as quickly as possible.

While Louise was changing her cousin's wet garments her reflections were most bitter. She had never known before how much wretchedness a commonplace day could hold within the limits of its brief hours. While she was still occupied with her little cousin, she heard Ralph Matthews's voice. He was saying civil things to her uncle and aunt. It was almost time for his train to go.

THE FATTED CALF

"Louise," called Mrs. Henderson, "can't you come down and bid our friend good-by?"

Susie was shivering, and Louise did not dare to leave her. She put her into her dress with nervous haste; her fingers trembled with excitement. She must see him before he went.

"In one moment, aunt Mary," she replied, but when that moment came he was gone. She was just in time to see him whisked out of sight in a basket phaeton, with Lilian Osgood by his side, driving her white pony with her accustomed grace. He was holding the red sunshade over her, and bending toward her, to say something which made her laugh.

That night Louise watched the sun set in a pink mist of clouds. The haycocks were all covered with their white nightcaps, the men were returning from their work. Some oxen and a load of hay passed slowly along the road. It was very peaceful and rural, "primitive," she thought — "primitive." She had a dull sense that the sun would continue to rise and shine and go down on this same tranquil scene for many long days in many long years for her.

To be miserable was a new feeling for Louise. She had one ray of hope. Perhaps, after all, she was mistaken, and Ralph did care for her. Possibly in those hours that he had spent with her uncle he had said something about his feeling for her.

"What did you and Mr. Matthews talk about, uncle Henry?" she asked shyly.

"Politics; he is on the right side. An excellent young man, with the best of principles. I have only one fault to find with him, and that is, he smokes. To be sure, he is on the wrong side with regard to the Prohibition Amendment, but he seems as anxious to stop the increase of intemperance as I am. We are all traveling on different roads, Louise, but we bring up at the same place at last."

"You dear thing," cried Louise, flinging her arms about his neck, "I wonder if you half realize how nice you are! a great deal nicer than any other man that I know."

Her uncle gave her a pleased, bewildered glance. He could not see the connection between his speech and its effect.

"Tea is ready," said her aunt, coming to the door. "It is literally tea to-night, — tea and crackers. I knew you would not be hungry, and we shall have to economize on our teas, and devote ourselves to eating up the remnants at dinner-time. They will last a week at least. That stupid Nora! However, the day went off very well; the dinner was not all that I could wish" —

"Or rather it was a little more than you could wish," put in Louise.

"And it did seem as if Christine Wiley brought out every bit of discord there was in our old piano; but the end of the afternoon made up for everything, for Ralph seems to have taken a great fancy to Lilian. I hope something will come of it. Nothing could be more suitable. They are both young, rich, and handsome, and she has always disliked East Bradfield. She is going to the mountains next week; perhaps they will meet there. Yes, on the whole, the day has been a success, although of course it would have been more gratifying if Ralph had not seen so obviously that we had 'killed the fatted calf' for him. I hope you are not as tired as I am, dear child, and that you have had a happy day."

Two evenings later, as Louise was again watching the sun go down, with the same sense of exasperation at its methodical clinging to its old ways when her world was so changed, Johnny brought her a letter.

"It is from Ralph Matthews," she thought. "He has had the grace to write and let us know of his safe arrival."

She tore open the envelope and hastily examined the contents. She read as follows: —

"MY DEAR MISS HENDERSON, — If you purposely avoided me at every turn yesterday; if you knew, as how could you help knowing, why I came to East Bradfield, and would not give me a chance to say what I was burning to say, you need not answer this letter. If, on the con-

THE FATTED CALF

trary, as I am bold enough at times to think, your coldness and seeming indifference were the result of circumstances, I will come again, and say it all, on my way back. But I will not come, Louise, unless I can come as your acknowledged lover. I will not be balked again at every turn by children, old maids, kind matrons, delightful elderly gentlemen, and pretty, flirtatious girls; I will not come unless " —

The rest of the letter brought a vivid blush to Louise's cheeks, and made her laugh and cry at once.

She sat up far into the night, composing a reply. It was six pages long. Then she tore it up, and began again; there was no need of expressing her whole heart in this ardent fashion. She wrote a shorter letter that pleased her no better, and then a still shorter one, and when she had finally struck out all that was unnecessary from her answer, only these four words were left : —

" You may come.   LOUISE."

TWO AUTHORS

Miss Ruth Pennell stood before the looking-glass that hung above her mahogany bureau, tying on her black straw bonnet. It had seen five summers' wear; but as Miss Pennell glanced at the gray hair it sheltered, she reflected, with a smile, that five years is not so great an age for a bonnet as is sixty-five for a woman. The mirror, in a frame of twisted gilt columns, with a life-size bunch of grapes across the top, was very old indeed, even for a mirror, and Miss Pennell envied it the power of keeping its good looks. She thought it a little unkind that when the lustre of the glass was as undimmed as in a former century, it should reflect so relentlessly the changes that time had brought its owner.

"How much I am growing to look like mother!" Miss Ruth said, as she caught a glimpse of her profile; then she remembered with something of a shock that she was nearly seventeen years older than her mother had been when she died. To be almost old enough to be one's own mother's mother is a little confusing; not that Miss Pennell objected to growing old, and indeed sixty-five seems almost like youth when compared with eighty-five, or even seventy-five; everything depends upon the point of view. To-day, however, Miss Ruth found it in her heart to wish for once that she and her bonnet were a little younger, for she had in prospect a two miles' walk to the village, whither she had been summoned to an afternoon tea given in honor of George Armitage, the author. Once she had hoped to be a great author herself, but that was long ago, when the mirror had been kinder to her than it was now, but life had been harder.

"After all, there are compensations in outgrowing one's illusions," she thought. "For if life is not such a triumphal progress as we fancy it will be when we are young, it is far broader and sweeter."

One of the things that made it so satisfying was the fact that across the continent a family of children were growing up who called her "aunt Ruth," incredible thought! It seemed so short a time since she was "Ruth" to every one, and other people, grave, dignified, elderly ladies in white caps, were "aunt" to her. At this point in her reflections she opened the upper drawer in her bureau and took out a pair of gray undressed kid gloves. They were a present that she had received on her last birthday, from her niece Ruth, and had come all the way from Illinois. She stroked them lovingly, for she was very fond of this niece, but she felt a little ashamed that she should take so much pleasure in the fact that they had five buttons.

"I believe I shall never grow old properly," she said. "I am afraid I am still a child at heart."

Miss Ruth slipped the gloves into her pocket to be worn later when she should reach the tea, and thriftily put on a pair of gray cotton ones. She locked the door and hid the key under the door-mat, that Harriet, her rosy-cheeked little maid-of-all-work, might find it there when she came home from school. She then started on her dusty walk to the village, holding up her gown carefully and thinking no more of the trials of the way, but turning her attention to the glories of the autumn foliage. She looked across the narrow green valley to the mountains which hemmed it in on either side, now all ablaze with glowing reds and yellows, against a background of dark green pines and hemlocks, and as she drew in a long breath of the bracing air she felt a keen delight in mere existence. It would have been joy enough simply to take a walk to the village on such an afternoon, but when she added the pleasure of seeing the author of "A New Hampshire Hillside," her cup of happiness was almost too full. She thought of her two little stories, and the few verses that had been published in a country newspaper long ago, and of her later poems that had been passed about in manuscript from neighbor to neighbor. If the composing of her simple verses had brought her so close to nature that the mere act of living became a daily joy, what would it be to have such keen sympathy with both nature and human nature as to be able to move thousands to tears and laughter?

She passed tidy white farmhouses with a golden wealth of pumpkins in the side yards, and strings of dried apples hanging in graceful festoons from the piazzas, and other farms over which she was obliged to shake her head in sorrowful disapproval, where the farmer's wife was "slack," and the apples were left in a disorderly heap. At last she reached the village and passed the brown church with the picturesque belfry, and the large summer hotel beyond it on the other side of the road. Another half mile brought her to the pleasant yellow house on the hill where George Armitage was entertained. She felt a little like a shy child, when she saw three grand carriages at the door that must have come all the way from the summer hotels at Jackson, for the inmates of the yellow house were city people, who belonged to Miss Ruth's world merely for three months in the year. She was troubled only for a moment, however.

"Mrs. Warren wouldn't have asked me if she hadn't wanted me to come," was her cheerful reflection, as she stepped into the square hall, with its polished oak floor and the large fireplace where a bright fire was blazing. The parlor was already full of guests who had come from far and near to get a glimpse of the great author. Miss Ruth stood in the doorway, letting her eyes wander from one face to another in the vain attempt to find a countenance that promised remarkable things. She had just made up her mind that the distinguished visitor had not arrived when her attention was caught by a cluster of ladies who had crowded around a tall, broad-shouldered young man. Could it be that this strong, athletic fellow, who seemed a mere boy in her eyes, was George Armitage? He was no more impressive than her nephew Tom. Indeed, he reminded her strongly of that dear but most unheroic individual. He had the same dark eyes and hair, and when he smiled his face lighted up in the same pleasant fashion.

At this point her hostess, resplendent

in black satin and jet, came forward to meet her.

"Dear Miss Pennell, how good of you to come all this way," she said cordially. "I want to present you to Mr. Armitage, for I know how much you like his book."

Miss Pennell shrank back as she glanced at the group of graceful girls in their pale pink and blue and white gowns.

"Don't introduce me, please," she said timidly. "He won't care to talk to an old woman like me when there are so many pretty young ladies here."

The attention of the hostess was distracted at this moment by the entrance of another guest, and Miss Ruth stepped up to the outskirts of the body guard that surrounded George Armitage. She was pushed close to him by a gayly dressed girl who elbowed her way through the crowd. The young lady had an affected manner, and as she shook hands with Mr. Armitage she remarked with effusion, "I want you to know that I was one of the first worshipers at the shrine of "A New Hampshire Hillside."

Miss Ruth could not help smiling, and at the same instant the young man looked up, and as his eyes met hers he smiled too.

That glance made her feel as if he were an old friend. "He is full of fun, like Tom," she thought.

Presently a member of the church sewing-circle, a bustling, elderly lady possessed of a kind heart but little tact, was struck with what she conceived to be Miss Pennell's forlorn position on the outskirts of Paradise.

"I am sure two authors ought to know each other," she said in a high, strident voice. "Mr. Armitage, let me make you acquainted with Miss Pennell. She is our poetess, although she may be too modest to mention it."

"I am very glad to meet a colleague," he returned with a friendly smile.

"And I am very glad to meet you because you look so much like my nephew Tom."

"Do I? How jolly! I hope he is a nice fellow."

"He is perfectly delightful."

"He is handsome, I trust," he inquired after one or two more questions.

"As I am his aunt, of course I am bound to say that he is handsomer than you are," Miss Ruth replied audaciously, for the spirit of mischief had seized her, and it almost seemed as if the veritable Tom were standing before her. "But there is a wonderful likeness," she admitted.

The gayly dressed girl with the affected manner stared at Miss Pennell with unaffected astonishment. And then a remarkable thing happened; so marvelous indeed that Miss Pennell could scarcely credit her senses. The great author, who had written a book that had moved thousands to tears and laughter, turned from the group of brilliant, gayly dressed girls, and his whole interest centred on the gray-haired old woman in the shabby bonnet. One of the elements of his power was an eye that could look beneath all outer disguises to the soul itself; and he had also the gift of quick sympathy and the ready tact that set the humblest interlocutor at ease. He asked Miss Pennell about her nephew and her home, and finally it happened, she could hardly tell how, that he invited himself to come and drink a cup of tea with her on the following afternoon.

"You must n't talk to me any more," she said, after the invitation had been asked for and received. "There are ever so many people here who have not seen you yet, and some of them have come all the way from the summer hotels at Jackson."

"Hang Jackson!" he exclaimed under his breath, and Miss Pennell thought him more like Tom than ever.

She moved away relentlessly notwithstanding, and began to talk to some of the members of her church. She was a favorite with them all, although most of her friends wished heartily that she would buy a new bonnet. But the bonnet for some reason seemed particularly suited to her this afternoon, and Miss Ruth was unusually charming, for there is nothing so becoming as happiness. She heartily enjoyed the occasion from beginning to end. It was the first time that she had been to a reception, and she could never understand afterwards why some people called them tiresome, for she thought this one even pleasanter than the church sewing-circle. She was introduced to some of the city people, and she found them as agreeable and as ready to talk as Mr. Armitage, although, of course, they could not have quite the same interest for her, as they were not authors. When it was all over she felt that she had never spent a pleasanter afternoon. She walked as far towards home as the post-office, where she waited for her neighbor, Deacon Scott, who had promised to drive her back when he came for the mail.

"I guess you 've had a real good time, for you look kind of smilin'," the deacon observed as he helped her into his wagon.

"Oh, I 've had a beautiful time. I only wish your wife had gone too."

"Wall, Elizy was dretful afraid of doin' the wrong thing. And then she had n't had a new bunnit for most three years, and she did n't like to go in among all them city people in her old duds, and she was afraid if the author saw her he 'd clap her into a book."

"She needn't have been afraid of that," said Miss Ruth, with a smile. "He isn't that kind of an author. He is real 'folksy,' and made me think of my nephew Tom."

"Du tell! Wall, I never calculated that Tom would be like any author, or any author like Tom. Look a' here, Miss Ruth. You ain't too proud to ride with an old feller like me, are you? I don't look much like one of your city swells, and a flour-barrel at the back of the wagon is kind of a curious companion for a lady who's be'n to a reception."

"Well, I guess when I'm too proud to ride with my old friends I'll go over to Jackson and board."

At this point one of the homeward-bound carriages with its fashionably dressed occupants drove past them. The girls bowed to Miss Ruth in a friendly way, and she returned the salutation with a half-laughing backward glance at the flour-barrel. There is no situation in life that cannot be gracefully met if one has natural ease and a sense of humor.

When Miss Pennell reached her little

house she entered in and took possession with something of the feeling of a princess in a fairy tale.

"Tell Eliza to come over as soon as she can," was her parting remark to the deacon, but Eliza needed no invitation; she had started to "come over" as soon as she saw the horse's head in the distance. She was a woman who had once been handsome, but whose face bore the stamp of hard work and depression.

"You ought to have gone, Eliza," Miss Ruth began at once.

"Well, as I told the deacon, I had too much pride. I don't mean that you did wrong to go," she hastened to add, "for you've traveled and been about, and then somehow you always look as if you belonged wherever you are, just as the flowers do, but it's different with me. I'm not a flower. I guess I'm a vegetable, and a very common sort at that. I should have looked like a fool, and I wasn't going there to be a show for others to laugh at, and to have 'em say, 'Look at Mrs. Deacon Scott! Doesn't she look as if she'd come out of the ark!' No, I may be lacking in some things, but I've a proper pride."

"But, Eliza, no one thought of laughing. They were all as kind as possible. Several of the sewing-circle were there. We didn't go to be seen, but to see. And Mr. Armitage was so nice. By the way, he is coming here to see me to-morrow afternoon."

"I want to know!"

"He really is. He proposed it himself. And if you would like to meet him," Miss Ruth added generously, "you can come over any time between four and five."

Mrs. Scott shook her head in a decided way.

"I can see him all I want to from the window," she remarked. "I don't feel any call to converse with authors; although I should like him to know how I admire his book. You might tell him that Mrs. Deacon Scott sat up until eleven o'clock at night to finish it. Perhaps it would please him to know that."

"I am sure it would," said Miss Ruth warmly.

"Now tell me what kind of sleeves the

ladies were wearing," said Mrs. Scott, "and how the house was fixed and what you had to eat."

When Miss Pennell had satisfied her neighbor on these points Mrs. Scott rose reluctantly.

"Well, I must go home now and get the deacon's supper," she remarked. "He isn't a mite particular, the deacon, but I do like to give him something hot. It's as good as a play to hear your account of the reception, Ruth, and a great deal better than being there myself."

Miss Ruth, however, could not agree to this, and she was left with a heartache as her friend closed the door. It seemed so sad to think of all the people in the world, who, simply through fault of temperament, missed the happiness that might be theirs. "Perhaps, though," she reflected presently, "Eliza 'll get more pleasure looking at him through the window than she would by seeing him, being the kind she is." It further occurred to her it was even possible that Eliza might be sorry for her sometimes, thinking of her as a lonely old maid. She threw back her head and laughed merrily at the idea of being pitied for so futile a reason. She glanced around her pleasant room, and had a feeling of pride and satisfaction in her cottage being all her own to do with as she liked.

Miss Pennell was in a flutter of excitement throughout the evening. She could not decide which teacup should have the honor of being at the service of George Armitage, and finally she had to call in the assistance of Harriet, the rosy-cheeked maid. They went together to the corner cupboard where Miss Pennell's best china was set forth in dainty array.

Harriet at once selected a gay teacup adorned with tiny pink-and-blue parrots sitting under a wonderful bower of rainbow-colored flowers against a white and gilt background.

"I like this one best," she announced, with the decision of youth.

"My brother brought it from China," Miss Pennell explained, "but somehow I have a fancy that Mr. Armitage will prefer one of my older cups," and she glanced from the sedate blue Canton china that had belonged to her father's mother to the fragile white-and-gilt tea-service that could boast an equally long pedigree on the other side of the house.

"If he's young he'll like the bright one best," said Harriet confidently.

Miss Ruth yielded somewhat doubtfully and found it a comfort to have the important matter settled. When she was ready to go upstairs for the night she stepped out of doors for a final look at the shadowy mountains lying vague and mysterious in the moonlight. But, alas! What had happened to the moon?

"Harriet," she said in a subdued voice, "come here a minute."

"Yes, Miss Ruth."

"Just look at those clouds and tell me what sort of weather we are likely to have to-morrow."

"I am sure we are going to have a northeaster, ma'am," Harriet answered uncompromisingly.

Indeed, it was only a few moments before the storm began. A wild night followed, and whenever Miss Pennell was wakened by a gust more furious than the last she could hear the swish of the rain against her windows. Her only hope was that the flood-gates would be emptied before the afternoon. The next morning, however, there were no signs of any abatement of the storm. Every mountain had vanished, and the world was a monotonous plane swathed in gray mist. The downpour did not begin to slacken until four o'clock, the hour at which her guest was to have come, and even then it was raining steadily.

"Well," Miss Pennell thought with a patient little sigh, "I suppose it is n't *for* me to have so much happiness. Yesterday ought to have been enough. But I should have liked to have him in this room just once! It would have seemed so much more furnished afterwards; there is no chance of his coming in such a storm, however, and he goes away early to-morrow morning."

At twenty minutes past four Miss Ruth resolutely took up a book. "I had better move away from that window and put my mind on other things," she said to herself. "Even if he wanted to come, Mrs. Warren wouldn't let him go out in this rain just to see an old woman like me; and of course, now I'm not there, his mind is all taken up with the next person. It's perfectly natural, and perhaps he wouldn't have come anyway; and if it had been pleasant and he hadn't come I should have been dreadfully disappointed, and so the rain may be a blessing in disguise."

Just then she heard the sound of approaching wheels. "No, I won't be such a fool as to go to the window again. It may be only Deacon Scott driving by."

A moment later there came a quick ring at the door. "It is probably the deacon or Eliza coming on some errand," she said to herself disingenuously, well knowing that they never rang.

"Mr. Armitage!" she exclaimed joyfully, as she opened the door, "I never expected you in such a storm."

"Does 'Tom' mind a trifle of this sort?"

"Not if he wants to do a thing very much; when he doesn't, I've known the gentlest kind of shower to keep him at home."

"You are right in saying that Tom and I are alike," he acknowledged, with a boyish laugh.

"Give me your mackintosh and umbrella. I hope you won't take cold. I shall never forgive myself if you do. You must come right in and get dry."

"What a cosy room!" he said, as he followed her into the parlor.

A bright fire was burning in the fireplace, flanked by brass andirons and an old-fashioned twisted brass fender. There was a large stand of plants at one of the south windows, and there were photographs, good and bad, against the cheerful yellow walls, and bookshelves filled with well-worn volumes. The room had individuality, like its owner, and a certain fresh flavor of the country.

George Armitage stood with his back to the fire, his tall figure thrown out in strong relief against the ruddy background, and as he talked genially, his eyes rested with pleasure on the sympathetic face of his hostess.

"You *are* like Tom!" she could not help exclaiming.

"You must show me his picture," he entreated, "for I want to have some idea how I look."

"Mr. Armitage, it is very rash of you to start me on the subject of my nephew, and as for his picture, I have a whole gallery of them, beginning when he was a baby and coming down to three years ago. Would you like to see the whole collection?" she inquired mischievously, "or will a sample do?"

"All. Nothing less will satisfy me."

She brought out her well-filled album and showed him Tom in long clothes, Tom in girl's dresses and in knickerbockers, and so on through a long succession of phases until she came to Tom at twenty-four. After a time they left this engrossing subject, and discussed photographs in general, and whether they gave a fair impression of the individual, and from this they went on to consider how much of the true inwardness of character is shown by a face.

"There are some people," said Miss Pennell, "who have beautiful natures whose bodies seem a perfect home for their souls, but there are others who are equally fine whose faces are like ugly masks. Once in a while you get a glimpse of the lovely spirit by means of a rare smile, or a glance from the eyes, but I am always sorry for such people. I feel as if they were like the unfortunate princes in the fairy-tales who have been imprisoned by some malicious spirit. You authors are able to get at the real person, and the reason I like 'A New Hampshire Hillside' is because you show the good there is under a rough exterior, and the happiness that can come into the humblest lives. There, I did not mean to talk to you about your book, for I know you must be very tired of that subject."

"I am never tired of such praise as yours. But, Miss Pennell, they tell me you write. I want to see what you have done."

"I only pretend to write. I can't really do it. I had two little stories printed in a newspaper long, long ago, when I was a girl, and five or six poems that are not poems; but I've been too wise to try to have them printed lately."

"I should like to see them just the same."

And so Miss Pennell brought out her old scrap-book, for it was well-nigh impossible to refuse this persuasive young man anything he asked.

"They are very bad," she said, shaking her head. "Once I used to think that I could write, but that was when I was a foolish girl."

"If they are like you" — he began, and then paused.

They sat there together in friendly silence, the man of the world who, young as he was, had already made an enviable reputation, and the woman who had always lived out of the world and had grown old without winning the least shadow of fame. The young man turned the yellow leaves of the scrap-book with a gentle touch, as if he found more there than was legible to the eye.

At last he looked up. "They are not very good," he said.

His voice was so friendly, that it took all the sting out of the words. It was if he had said, "You are right, but it does n't matter. I like you just as much as if you had talent. What we call talent is of very little consequence anyway."

"I used to care so for it when I was young," she murmured, "but now I don't care at all. I simply enjoy what other people can do. And yet it makes me happy to scribble bad verses, because it teaches me to see nature with new eyes. I am glad I have tried, for failing has taught me to appreciate the best."

"You seem very happy," he said thoughtfully.

"Yes, I am."

"Are n't you ever lonely here in winter?"

"No. It is even more beautiful than it is at this season, for the mountains are covered with snow, and so are the pines and hemlocks, and there is such freshness and crispness in the air. Besides, in the winter we have more time to be sociable, and I read a great deal, and I get letters twice a week from my people in Illinois. Then there is July to look forward to — when I shall see them again."

"Do you never spend the winter with them?"

"I spent one winter there, but although they were very kind, it is hard to adjust one's self to the ways of other people after living all alone in a whole house; and Illinois is so flat; I was homesick for my mountains."

Mr. Armitage went over to the window, and stood watching the driving mist which was beginning to roll away from the hills. "I don't wonder you like your view," said he.

"Isn't it grand? I am so glad it is showing itself to you in part. There is always something new to be seen from these windows. It is like reading an interesting book without an end. Do you wonder I am never lonely? And yet I used to be lonely and discontented when I was a girl. I don't think scenery is so satisfying when you are young. It is strange we are so seldom contented when we have the most to enjoy. I am always glad," she added impulsively, "when I come across some one like you who has success and happiness early; for to have youth and all the other good gifts together is a beautiful thing."

His face changed. "I am not happy," he confessed. "I should be very glad if I could enjoy life as you can. Of course I don't mean that I don't get a lot of surface pleasure out of it, but when there is a very hard thing in your life that you have got to bear, nothing else seems any good."

Miss Pennell was the sort of woman to whom secrets are told, and she knew that a word from her would encourage this young man to give her his whole story, but she had an instinctive shrinking from receiving confidences, and so she merely said, "I am so sorry," and went to summon Harriet to bring in the tea. The young girl came at once, bristling with importance from her long brown braids to her shiny, squeaking new shoes. But, alas for the little maid! Mr. Armitage sipped his tea not only in utter unconsciousness of her, but likewise of the teacup!

"I hope the hard thing in your life can be changed some time," Miss Ruth said softly, after Harriet had left the room.

"There are some things that can never be changed."

"Yes, I know. There is death; and sometimes we lose our friends in other ways, which is harder still. But we can change. We can live through things and learn to bear them. Sometimes it seems as if a great tidal wave had swept everything before it, and changed the whole world, but after a time there comes—peace. And when we have reached this point, in one way it does n't so much matter what happens to ourselves, for we are so small a part of the great scheme; and in another way we feel that it matters infinitely more, and that we must do our share without shirking, to help on the rest. And when we get to be old, we can look back and see how the trials take their part in the whole plan."

They were both silent for a time after this, for shyness overtook them, and presently Miss Pennell changed the subject and talked of commonplace things.

"Here comes my carriage," George Armitage said at last. He had resumed his usual cheerful manner, and nodded brightly to Mrs. Warren, who had driven over for him herself. The rain had stopped in the valley, but it was still showering on the mountains, and their summits were veiled in a haze of golden mist, behind which the sun seemed struggling to come through. Miss Ruth looked at the golden glory and thought it a fitting ending to her happy day.

"I have had such a beautiful time," she said, as she gave Mr. Armitage's hand a warm pressure. "You have given me great pleasure. Nothing has ever happened to me so like a story book. I have always wanted to know a real author, and now I have seen my Carcassonne."

"It is not for me to say it is a very poor kind of Carcassonne so long as I am like Tom," he returned.

After he had gone she sat gazing at the ever clearing western sky, with a smile on her lips. "I have had such a happy day! Such a happy day!" she repeated over and over again. And then her face grew grave. "Poor boy! I wonder what is troubling him!" she thought. Her woman's curiosity awoke, and for the moment overcame her principles. "Of course it was right for me not to let him tell me," she said to herself. "It was only a momentary impulse, and he would have been sorry afterwards that he had confided in a stranger. But how I should like to know his story! And now I never shall."

The Riverside Press
CAMBRIDGE, MASSACHUSETTS, U. S. A.
ELECTROTYPED AND PRINTED BY
H. O. HOUGHTON AND CO.

www.ingramcontent.com/pod-product-compliance
Lightning Source LLC
Chambersburg PA
CBHW032120230426
43672CB00009B/1806